BONFIRE
THE CHESTNUT GENTLEMAN

SUSAN RABY-DUNNE

Monday Morning Writers Group

www.mondaymorningwritersgroup.com

Published by MMWG, (Monday Morning Writers Group).
First Edition

Library and Archives Canada Cataloguing in Publication

Raby-Dunne, Susan, 1954-
        Bonfire : the chestnut gentleman / Susan Raby-Dunne.

Story of the writing of John McCrae's poem In Flanders fields.
Includes bibliographical references.
ISBN 978-0-9877856-3-3

        1. McCrae, John, 1872-1918--Fiction. 2. World War, 1914-1918--
Fiction. I. McCrae, John,1872-1918 [In Flanders fields] II. Title.

PS8635.A237B66 2012   C813'.6   C2012-906665-6

Book design by Dean Pickup and Susan Raby-Dunne
Bonfire illustration by Penny Corradine
Author's photo by Monique de St.Croix
Printed and bound in Canada by Friesens

For my son, Rowan.
For all my soldiers, on this side and the other,
and for Jack.

ACKNOWLEDGEMENTS

I wish to thank all the people on this long road who have inspired, supported and indulged me and helped me learn my subject: Bev Dietrich and Kathleen Wall, at the McCrae House Museum/Guelph Museums in Guelph, Ontario; Piet Chielens, at the In Flanders Fields Museum in Ypres/Ieper, Belgium; Charlotte Descamps, for her wonderful hospitality several times at "research central," otherwise known as Varlet Farm B & B in Poelcapelle, Belgium; WWI guide, Les Moores for touring me around the Boulogne and Wimereux areas at the beginning of this journey; Tim Cook, WWI historian at the Canadian War Museum in Ottawa, Ontario; Major Marc George, at the Royal Artillery Museum in Shilo, Manitoba; the staff at Talbot House in Poperinghe, Belgium; writer Joseph Boyden, author of award-winning WWI novel *Three Day Road*; Dianne Graves, author of *A Crown of Life: The World of John McCrae*; and historians Robin Barker-James, Victor Taboika and Dave Love.

I'm especially indebted to Frans Hoijtink, Patrick van Wanzele and De Diggers battlefield excavation group of Ieper, Belgium, for helping me tap into the physical reality of WWI. I'm also very appreciative of the hospitality Frans Hoijtink and Mel Searston have shown me at their home beside the Essex Farm Cemetery.

I'm grateful for my teachers and friends Ed Tick and Kate Dahlstedt of Soldier's Heart, for teaching me about war trauma, the *invisible wound* through the ages, and how it can be healed.

I'd like to give special thanks to my precious writers and publishing group, MMWG, (Monday Morning Writers Group), for the feedback and for their support and tolerance of my obsession lo these last eight years: Sheelagh Matthews, Marika d'Ailly, Angela Simmons, Dorothy Irwin, and past members Clover Slusar and Evonne Smulders.

I would like to thank my editor, Rachel Small, and proofreader, Paula Kroeker, and talented book design guy, Dean Pickup.

I send out a special thanks to radio and television host Charles Adler, for his enthusiastic support of me and my projects ever since 'the McCrae journey" began in 2006, and for his support of our military and respect for our Canadian military history.

I give grateful thanks to friends who commune with the otherworldly realms on my behalf: Fredrick, Sarie Hobbs and Angela Ramson and my friend and Reiki Master, Sandy Day, for supporting me unconditionally and soothing my spirit.

Last, but far from least, I would like to thank Seamus Dunne, my sister Karen Robinson (for proofreading, too) and my family for their forbearance over the years of this all-consuming interest in John McCrae and WWI.

PROLOGUE

I was known throughout Quebec as Bonfire, *Fox Hunter Extraordinaire*. But that was before my owner, Doctor Todd, gave me to his friend, The Major, in the fall of 1914. I was upset at first. One never likes change and everyone knows that we horses are, by definition, creatures of habit. But it wasn't long at all before I realized that I would never be in better hands.

Doctor Todd was fond of all his fine, fox-hunting horses; but The Major loved me. No, love is not too strong a word. As much as a human can love an animal, that man adored me. I don't know why. Maybe it was the trying circumstances we found ourselves in during the spring of 1915, on the road to Ypres in Flanders. Nothing brings creatures closer than war.

Actually that's not fair. Our friendship began before that, in the giant tent city called Camp Valcartier, Quebec, before we even got on that ship bound for England. It all started before we ever walked up the plank into the ship called Saxonia, which would take us to the mucky plain near the strange collection of upright stones called Stonehenge.

My owner, Doctor Todd, wasn't a bad sort. But if you were to ask me if I preferred galloping hell-bent-for-election cross-country over hedges, ditches and brick walls after a poor, terrified fox or going for a relaxing hack with the gentle Major, I'd have to say the latter. And getting fed a pound or two of blackberries into the bargain? Who could resist? That was in France after the terrible battle The Major and I were in, but I'm getting ahead of myself.

It all started with Camp Valcartier. Doctor Todd shipped me from his stable to that place by train, a short but stressful journey. We were crammed into grubby livestock cars like kippers in a can–horses of all qualities and descriptions, even mules! I couldn't imagine where we were all going.

The other train cars were full of excited, and, for the most part, deliriously happy young men. Such chatter! Such bravado!

I couldn't understand why Doctor Todd would send me away. I'd never received anything but the highest praise from everyone for my prowess as a hunter and jumper, and let's face it, for my good looks as well. Whenever Doctor Todd entertained guests for any reason, they were brought down to the stables to see me. In fact, if Doctor Todd didn't bring them down to the barn of his own volition, they inevitably would ask, "May we see Bonfire?" and he'd bring them down regardless.

Children in twos and threes would be led round the yard on my back. I didn't mind that actually. But if the visitors were adults, Marjory, Doctor Todd's wife, would ride me over a course of jumps by way of showing off. The guests would applaud. Several asked if I was for sale and the answer was always a resounding, "Never! We could never part with him."

So why he would suddenly pack me onto a train with other horses, many of whom were of dubious quality and character, was a mystery and a source of anxiety for me. Where could I be going? And why?

Part One

Camp Valcartier

ONE

Camp Valcartier was a sprawling military camp thrown together by the blustering, steel-jawed Minister of Militia, Sam Hughes, for the purpose of training scores of Canadian soldiers, which certainly had everything to do with the excitement in the air. It was not far from Quebec City, and had been cleared of forest in record time and set up to accommodate new recruits, which numbered about thirty thousand by the time I arrived.

The first time I laid eyes on The Major was in early September, 1914. Just before that, a short, bowlegged man with an enormous moustache who was called Dinky behind his back, but Colonel Morrison to his face, had hidden me behind the officers' mess tent. I was being held by a private called Dodge. Dodge was a small, wiry Englishman with little red veins across his nose and cheeks. He was older than most of the young soldiers, and he kindly fed me oats and kept me amused for half an hour or so.

Dodge was a farrier by trade, and made a production of examining my feet and shoes, muttering all the while that this was not right and that was at the wrong angle and that he would never have used these types of nails. I didn't mind because he was genuinely interested and concerned about my feet.

Doctor Todd used to say, "No foot, no horse." If a horse's feet weren't well taken care of, he'd be of no use for anything at all. I noticed many of the riff-raff in the train car with me were unshod, had cracked hooves or had hooves that hadn't been trimmed in months and had started to curl.

As I stood there, I could hear all the goings-on in the mess tent: the clatter of plates, cups and cutlery as about twenty officers were served their lunch. There was much laughter and bold speculation about how they were going to lay a licking on the Hun, whatever or whomever that was.

Then I heard several men coming out of the mess tent, and Dinky's head appeared around the corner. He nodded to Dodge, who led me around to the front of the tent. All the men oohed and aahed as I strode out.

Now I'm really not vain, but compared to a lot of the ragtag mob I saw at Valcartier, let's just say I stood out. I had never seen such a collection of nags in my life—mangy, lame geldings, heavily pregnant mares sold as suitable mounts for soldiers, aged ponies that were supposedly young horses still growing. All manner of criminals calling themselves horse sellers and traders had sold herds of such rabble to the CEF, or Canadian Expeditionary Force.

There were also stout, tough and most unattractive horses shipped out from the West referred to as cayuses. They were much shorter than I and quite homely indeed, but at least most of them could be ridden. That is, they wouldn't roughly unload their riders into the talcum powder-like Valcartier dirt. Perhaps one horse in ten was worth the oats and hay he was being fed. I admit, the food was surprisingly good for a hastily thrown together military training camp.

And yes, I stood out: sixteen hands two inches, a coat of burnished copper (hence the name, Bonfire), two sparkling rear white stockings and a white star. I was an Irish hunter. All the soldiers were impressed but The Major was the most excited one of the lot. I realized he was to be my man and that Doctor Todd had given me to him as a gift.

Dinky Morrison said, "Todd was going to bring him down personally in a horse box, but he was called away with an emergency of some sort so he had to put him on the train."

While the other soldiers oohed and aahed, The Major positively beamed and said nothing at all except, "Well," and "Well well." He walked around and around me and ran his gentle hand along my back, flank and over my rump. He made my skin squiggle several times and laughed an infectious laugh each time I flinched.

Then he stood right in front of me and scratched my forehead. I had no idea how he knew that this was one of my two favourite things. My other favourite thing was having my ears rubbed, inside and out. To my amazement, he discovered that within minutes as well. I soon realized that leaving Doctor Todd's stable might not have been a bad thing after all.

The Major stood in front of me and smiled like a foolish boy. He was an artillery officer and older than everyone around except Dinky, who was older yet. At this point I resolved to call The Colonel Colonel Morrison rather than Dinky. Despite his small stature, Colonel Morrison had a distinctly commanding presence. I felt Dinky was just not properly respectful. Also, The Major never ever called him that nickname, so I would take my cues from The Major.

Both The Major and Colonel Morrison were quite old for soldiers in my estimation. I knew both men were in the artillery because they had tiny metal cannons on the fronts of their hats. The Major was tall and slim, about eighteen hands high, I reckoned–I guess that's six feet tall in human terms–and he had sparkling blue eyes of a gem-like quality I'd never seen before. Laughing eyes.

I don't know what possessed me, but I decided to show him a trick I used to do at Doctor Todd's stable with the boy groom there. I reached out and took off his hat, held it high out of his reach and then dropped it in the dirt. Instantly I regretted it. I squinted my eyes shut and waited for an angry roar, but all I heard was his deep, resonant laugh. I opened my eyes, and soon everyone else laughed too.

All he said was, "I think we're going to be great friends, you and I." He stooped and picked up his cap. I can't tell you how warm my whole insides became with that. I don't even know what the feeling I had would be called, only that it was very pleasing.

I soon realized nothing was certain at Valcartier. As The Major led me away, I heard a young soldier call out, "Sir? Now what are you going to do with the bay?" which I took to mean he already had a horse. My heart sank because I didn't know who this bay was, and if my position was insecure because of him.

The Major replied, "We'll see, Lex. Don't know yet. Maybe this big red won't be as good. I'll say one thing, son. He already has the advantage in looks, and more importantly, in temperament."

I wondered what he meant by that but was soon to find out.

And calling Lex "son." The Major seemed to be very caring, and I made up my mind right then to go to any length to prove to the kind Major that I was the horse he should keep for . . . well, for whatever this whole exercise was about, whatever it was. And if the bay was anything like the other rabble I saw around me in this place, there'd be no problem.

I may have been overconfident.

Nearly all the horses at Valcartier were tied in lines outside, but that wasn't good enough for The Major. He led me to a tent/stable affair that he had made and there inside was the bay, tied with his rear end to the open door.

The Major led me in and tied me beside the bay, who was almost as tall as I and very shiny and fit. He had a distinctive, curved white sliver of a new moon on his forehead. I endeavored to greet him nose to nose as we horses do, but all he did was pin his ears back and bare his teeth. I pulled away, sure he was going to bite me. Ill-tempered nag!

The Major took off his hat and swatted the bay on his rump. "Quit!" he said sharply. The bay took a step to the side, away from me, and his ears returned to a somewhat upright position. Still, he stood and glowered at me. "You're making my decision easier, Thor," sang The Major.

Hmph. Thor, I thought, that's quite a grand name for such a surly beast.

"I hope I can leave you two here without supervision and you'll not scrap." He studied us for a moment and then saw someone coming and turned to him. "Dodge. The very man. Keep an eye on these two while I conduct medical exams this afternoon, will you?"

"Yes, sir."

And that's when I was quite surprised to realize that The Major was not only an artillery officer but a doctor as well. He went into his own tent beside ours and came out again with a copper box, which he set on a table outside. I turned my head as far as I could and watched with one eye.

The copper box had all sorts of drawers, which he pulled out and checked. Inside were little brown bottles, vials, scissors, needles and tubes, along with white cloth bandages in rolls, gauze and thread for stitches. Very much like the kit Doctor Thomas, my veterinarian at Doctor Todd's, had.

I was comforted by the thought that The Major was a doctor too. Surely there couldn't be much difference between doctoring horses and people. If I was very good and he picked me over the sullen brown horse sulking beside me, I would be in good hands.

He shouldered the copper box and came to stand behind our tent. He looked at us, from one to the other, deep in thought. Dodge was cleaning horse brushes beside our tent.

"Dodge, I seriously need you to keep an eye on these two until the big red fellow here settles in. Thor was fixing to bite him earlier, and I don't think he's changed his opinion of our new guest yet."

Dodge said, "Yes, sir," as he dragged a wooden box of brushes, currie combs, leg wraps and so on from the side of our tent to the back of it, where he could see us.

"I'll be back in a couple of hours. Listen, Dodge. Tomorrow is Sunday, and after church parade, I'm going to do some riding and start making my decision between these two. I want you to have my tack ready and make sure everything is in order with both of these horses. Alright?"

"Yes, sir," Dodge said with happy enthusiasm, and I had the feeling this Dodge fellow was one of those who are born to serve. "What will you do with the one you don't take?"

"Young Helmer doesn't have a mount yet, so the loser will probably go to him. Whichever one keeps up the best with Colonel Morrison's horse, King, will have to be my choice." The Major studied us again for a moment. "Right. I'm off," he said with a determined tone, and he strode away.

TWO

Dodge began to brush me vigorously with a stiff-bristled brush, which felt positively heavenly but caused my lips to twitch in that embarrassing, involuntary and undignified way. Thor noticed and sneered at me with a sidelong, squinty-eyed dagger of a look. Then Dodge moved to my rump.

"Oh, dear oh dear." He shook his head. "Look at the backs of your socks! I'll need to wash those." My rear white socks had gotten stained with green manure in the crowded train car. "Back in a moment, lads. You behave yourselves," he said sternly. "I need some water." And then to himself he muttered quietly, "They should be alright for a couple of minutes." I wasn't so sure, and I looked at Thor to try to gauge his mood.

Dodge picked up a tin bucket and disappeared from sight. No sooner had he gone than Thor, on my left, began to pull on his halter shank and swing his rear end away and to the left. He managed to turn himself so his front end was almost facing me, and like lightning, he raised his right leg and struck down hard with his hoof, glancing down my upper left leg with an excruciating blow.

There was nothing I could do but pull back as hard as I could to get away from him. My lead shank stretched and snapped, and I got myself out of there and away from that demon. By the time Dodge returned moments later, I was fifty feet away. I stood and trembled with the pain, and Dodge dropped the bucket and came running.

"Jesus, Mary and Joseph! Can I not turn my back?! Damn it, you've broken your lead and your halter too. The Major will be furious."

Dodge grabbed another shank and strode angrily toward me. "And we thought YOU were the quiet one." And then from my away side, he saw the rivulets of blood run down and pool on the ground. His face fell. "Oh, no." He came around and saw the wound. He slowly turned and I could feel his anger. He stared back at Thor, who was now nonchalantly munching hay from the manger. "I swear. I swear if I had a loaded gun right now . . ."

Dodge tied me to a tree, ran and got the bucket with what remained of the water in it and grabbed some field dressings from his own kit. He tried to stop the bleeding with compression, and when the young lieutenant Lex Helmer appeared in the distance, Dodge hollered, "Lieutenant Helmer. Lieutenant!"

Lex heard him and came running. He saw my leg. "What in the world?" A flap of skin about eight inches long had been peeled back from the blow and hung off my leg dripping a steady stream of blood.

Dodge said, "I only went for a bucket of water and Thor must have kicked him. Struck him with a front foot. Can you please get The Major? He needs treatment, probably stitches, and the sooner the better before the flies get at it."

Moments later The Major appeared with Lex. He had the copper box and strode up to Dodge and me. Dodge hung his head.

"I'm so sorry, Major. Aagh. I'm so sorry. I only went to get water to wash his socks and Thor must have—"

The Major interrupted him tersely. "Never mind Dodge. Never mind. Just go and get more water. Clean water. Go."

The Major quickly took off his tunic and spread it out on the ground. Then he knelt and started taking things out of the copper box and laying them out on the tunic. He got out thread for stitching and a huge needle, bandages, a bottle of antiseptic and scissors. He stood and spoke to me.

"Well, Bonfire, that's a fine welcome. And I was going to ride you tomorrow. I don't know if you'll be fit enough for anyone now. Doubtful. At least not before our departure date, if at all. " He sighed heavily.

My heart sank as he began to soak up the blood with a field dressing. Bonfire, Fox Hunter Extraordinaire, would have no chance to prove himself. Washed up before he even got started.

Lex went into the tent and studied Thor. Then he knelt and looked at the front of his right hoof. It was clearly bloodstained. Lex stood up and stared at the horse.

"You're a devil," he said. "Not fit for anyone or any job in this army, I don't think."

Dodge reappeared with a full bucket of water, and The Major washed the wound and then liberally dabbed antiseptic on it, which stung sharply and made my eyes water. Then Dodge held me while The Major stitched. He cut off the torn flap of skin with scissors because it would only shrivel and die now without blood supply. Several stitches later I was patched up.

The Major started to lead me back to my tent but stopped.

"Private Dodge. Get that animal out of my sight."

"Yes, sir." Dodge quickly undid Thor's lead shank and backed him out of the tent. "Where will I take him sir?"

"Over the cliff and into the river sounds like the obvious choice."

Dodge studied The Major's face. Was he serious? The Major smiled weakly and sighed.

"Just tie him up . . . outside. Outside and away from any other horses from now on. Is that clear, Dodge?"

"Yes, sir." Dodge led Thor away, annoyed and muttering under his breath. "You'd be a fine animal in every way. But fit for no man with that nasty temperament. Fit for no man at all."

If a horse could smile, Thor smiled as Dodge led him away. He'd badly injured the interloper and perhaps gotten out of a hard day's riding after church parade as well.

The Major led me into my spot and gave me a big scoop of oats, which I appreciated very much. These soldiers didn't yet know about the legendary Bonfire appetite. The Major examined the wound at length and talked to me the whole time. He apologized and said he'd do his best to make it right. He stayed with me until the dark started to descend.

"Well, I'm off to bed, Bonfire. I hope your leg has improved by morning . . . but I doubt if it will be." He patted me on the neck. Then as he walked away, he said quietly to himself, "I'll be afraid to look tomorrow."

I didn't sleep well at all. My leg throbbed with pain. In the morning, it had swollen and was hot and ached with the beginnings of infection, probably from Thor's filthy hoof.

The Major came out first thing, with Private Dodge trailing behind him, and had a look at it.

"Oh, dear. What a mess." He looked into my eyes and held my head in his hands. "We'll do our best, Bonfire, won't we, Dodge?"

"We will, sir," said Dodge forlornly.

The Major spun around with purpose and spoke. "Now, Private Dodge, saddle up that bay. I will take him for the ride of his life after church parade. Never mind raising his leg to strike–he won't have the energy to raise his head when I'm through with him."

Dodge couldn't conceal his surprise and started to open his mouth. The Major put up his hand.

"Thor is my original horse and the horse I've been given. I'll have to give it my best effort before I rule him out, especially now that Bonfire's been injured. Believe me, Dodge, I don't like it either. And I'm dreading having to tell Todd what has happened to his gift."

The Major walked away but then stopped. He turned around, thoughtfully stroking his chin.

"Major?" said Dodge.

"We've got one week before we sail. What about that magic horse elixir of yours? Your old sergeant major's mixture?"

"Oh, yes!" Dodge clapped his hand to his forehead as he remembered. "Sergeant Major Fraser's Magic Horse Liniment?"

Dodge had served with Fraser in the Boer War.

"That concoction. Whatever it is, I know you swear by it, so slather it on. It can't hurt. Slather it on and pray for a miracle, for both of us. I don't want to be stuck with that miserable bay, and I doubt if you do either."

"No, sir, I do not. I certainly do not."

The Major walked away, and Dodge rummaged in the tack trunk and came out with a clear quart bottle, three quarters full of honey-coloured oil. He knelt down beside me with a clean cloth and poured a healthy dollop on it. I squinted and braced for a sting, but it didn't hurt at all. I bent my head down and smelled it. Not too bad. An unusual but not unpleasant smell.

"Don't fuss with it, you," Dodge said to me. "It'll be just the thing to get this healing. The Major is of a scientific mind and has always been skeptical of these home remedies. Hmm. He must be desperate. And to resort to this he must really want you, Master Bonfire. Let us pray for success."

Dodge slathered it on and covered it with a fresh bandage. I have to say, the pain seemed to diminish like magic. Or was it my imagination? I was desperate too–desperate to take the place of that bay hellion. I had no idea what was in store, but I felt it wouldn't matter, as long as I was with The Major.

Dodge held me on a long shank outside and let me graze wherever I liked for a couple of hours. While we were out there, The Major thundered past on Thor, who was really starting to sweat. They came around twice more in the next hour, and the last time, Thor had foam on his neck and was sopping wet.

Later The Major returned leading Thor, who was soaking wet from nose to tail. His sides heaved and his head hung down to his hooves. He was exhausted. The Major walked up to Dodge.

"Untack him and walk him until he's dry. Water him once his breathing's back to normal. I don't know if that did any good, but he seems to have lost most of that cockiness for now anyway."

Dodge nodded worriedly toward me. "You don't want him back in with . . ."

"Oh, no. Definitely not. He's lost that privilege."

Dodge took Thor's saddle and bridle off and put a halter on him. Then they went off walking. Perhaps I'm soft, but I did feel a little sorry for that knackered bay horse. He had not even the strength or the will to give me a dirty look as they walked away.

* * *

My leg felt better and better as the day went on. When evening came, I had a great sleep, and first thing the next day, The Major and Dodge walked up and led me out of the tent. Dodge held me and The Major removed the bandage. For the first time, I noticed his breathing. I could hear it; a rasping sound that crackled and squeaked in his chest. He knelt beside my leg.

"I'll be damned. It's noticeably better." He put the flat of his hand over the wound without touching it. Very little heat." He leaned down and sniffed my leg. "Smells okay too. I believe the infection is almost gone! Amazing!"

He stood and brushed off his knees and beamed. "Amazing, Dodge!"

Dodge shrugged and smiled broadly, resisting the urge to say, "I told you so."

"Right. Get him walking. Walk him all around the place. Not too fast, but let's get his blood circulating and that will speed the healing. Hmm. I might be taking him across the pond after all. Keep putting that stuff on. Just keep it up."

"Will do, sir," said Dodge.

The Major's smile warmed my heart and made me hopeful. Across the pond. What pond, I wondered?

"Bring him over to me after lunch. I'll check his leg again and then you can tie him up outside the examination tent for a change. I'll walk him back when I'm finished for the day. I've been going hammer and tongs with these recruits. I put through twenty-two yesterday myself. Only had to turn away three, one clinically blind! Don't know what he was thinking. A blind gunner!"

Both the Major and Dodge laughed, and the laughter made The Major cough.

"There was a fellow from Montreal who had the beginnings of tuberculosis, and the third, from out in the west, Manitoba, had some other kind of chest problem."

"Like your asthma, sir?" Dodge looked suddenly uncomfortable, like he'd misspoken.

The Major looked at him, pausing before he spoke. "No. Not asthma. Perhaps emphysema. He was a very heavy smoker–yellow fingers, yellow moustache and dreadful breath. Not asthma anyway. Well," he brushed off his knees again, "I'm off and I'll see you two after lunch."

* * *

After The Major had gone, Dodge led me slowly through the camp for the first time. I was stiff at first, but the further we went, the more limber my leg felt. It was anything but boring, I can tell you. Such activity! Hundreds of men and horses. All sorts of drills taking place. Groups of men ran by as part of fitness training. Other groups did jumping jacks or ran hollering at swinging bags of straw with bayonets and tried to stab them with various degrees of accuracy.

We walked behind a shooting range, where men lay on the ground and shot their rifles at distant targets. There was a lot of yelling and cursing from the drill sergeants in charge.

We walked by a huge corral, where several men were working with green horses. All sorts of bucking, bolting and rearing up going on.

Wild things altogether. What a display! I saw a horse rear up and fall right over backwards with his rider, who managed to throw himself sideways just in time to miss being crushed.

We passed a sea of small, white bell tents, perhaps two hundred of them in neat rows. Beside my stall, The Major slept in one of his own, just like the common recruits.

By the time we'd walked for an hour, my leg felt almost as good as new, as if it hadn't been injured at all. We came upon a gathering of army chaplains. Just then, up came the imposing Minister of the Militia, Sam Hughes, on his own horse. He was a big man with an iron jaw, bushy black eyebrows and fierce eyes. He dismounted and spoke to the chaplains.

Dodge backed me into a thicket of bushes, out of the Minister's line of view. But we could see and hear everything.

"Men, you have a very important role in the Canadian Expeditionary Force, and that is to keep the morale high and be a light for these soldiers–to hold up the light of God and keep these men on the straight and narrow. God is on our side in this fight, and you must

Valcartier - Brigadier Sir Sam Hughes inspecting instructional staff - 1914

remind the men of this at any and every opportunity, especially whenever you see doubt!"

Minister Hughes was very red in the face and emphatic. The chaplains looked at each other with sidelong glances and subtle questioning looks. One of them in the front row raised his hand and spoke.

"Sir?"

Minister Hughes walked up to him and squinted at his badge.

"Question . . . Chaplain Bridgewater?" the Minister boomed, saliva spraying out on the Chaplain.

"Yes, sir." Chaplain Bridgewater blinked as though facing a strong wind. "Will we be allowed to carry handguns, sidearms?" he asked. "Sir?"

"You will not! Not at all!" the Minister roared. Then he narrowed his eyes, leaned in confidentially and said quietly, "But I do suggest you each carry a bottle of castor oil."

"Ye . . . yes, sir," Chaplain Bridgewater said. The chaplains looked at each other again as Minister Hughes got up on his horse again and rode away. "Castor oil, you say," said Bridgewater as the minister rode out of earshot, and then several of the chaplains fell about, laughing uproariously.

I thought to myself, I'm afraid the Minister might be a couple of hay bales short of a wagonload. Dodge led me away, chuckling to himself. It occurred to me suddenly that all this must be leading to a war somewhere. The Minister had said, "God is on our side in this fight." A fight across the pond?

Someday The Major and I would be indebted to the eccentric Minister of the Militia. But that would be later, after the great battle.

Captain Colebourn and Winnie the bear, Valcartier, 1914

All these things were interesting and thought provoking, though worrying. But the most amazing thing we saw was veterinary officer Captain Colebourn, and his mascot: a baby black bear named Winnie!

I couldn't believe my eyes. The little bear stood on her hind legs, just like a human. Valcartier was full of surprises.

We came up a soft dirt path toward a group of big, rectangular white tents. There was The Major with a pipe in his mouth at a table outside, filling out and signing forms. He looked up and saw us and his face lit up. He set down his pipe in an ashtray.

"Attestation papers by the bushel. Almost fifteen thousand soldiers attested so far, Dodge. Pledging their military services to King and

Empire. All to be signed, stamped and dated. The medical exam is the least of it."

He sighed and then stamped several papers with a little oval stamp that said, "1st Bde. (brigade), Canadian Field Artillery." Stamp, stamp, stamp.

"There. That's enough for now. Until after lunch. Leave Bonfire here with me and you can go, Dodge. I'll bring him back before dinner. Off you go. Have a look at Thor's hind right, will you? It seemed as if he might be on the verge of losing a shoe after yesterday."

Dodge led me to a horse line a few feet away and tied my lead shank to it. I didn't even want to hear the name, Thor. It reminded me that although my leg seemed to be healing, it wasn't healed yet. My position still was not certain. A wave of fear passed through me.

The Major stood up and put on his tunic. He knocked the stinky contents of his pipe into the ashtray and put the pipe in his pocket. Then he picked up the copper box from another table and came to where I was tied. He set the box down and knelt beside me, removing the bandage.

"It's looking good, Bonfire. Excellent progress." He replaced the bandage and stood up. "If this continues I'm going to ride you on Friday. Not far. Not hard. Just a little test. OK?" He looked right in my face and gave my forehead a scratch. "C'mon. We'll go for a stroll."

The Major took a sandwich out of his bag, and we walked away from the tents toward the river. After he'd finished it, he stopped and fished an apple out of his tunic pocket.

"Where are my manners?" He took one bite of the apple and fed the rest to me. It was a very welcome treat. We walked down to the Jacques Cartier River, and I had a long, delicious drink out of it.

As we walked, The Major sang a song that sounded very cheery, despite the dire words.

"The minstrel boy to the war has gone, / In the ranks of death you'll find him."

His beautiful, deep voice was precisely on key, for which I was grateful. Dr. Thomas, our veterinarian, used to sing or whistle continuously and not on key at all. Never. Not even close. It was positively painful to hear.

We walked by a group of young soldiers wrestling–practising for hand-to-hand combat, I supposed.

"You're dead!" hollered one.

"Naw, you're dead," shouted the other.

They seemed to be having more fun than anything, and two who were wrestling collapsed with laughter. The Major became thoughtful and serious watching them. He turned to me and stroked my neck.

"They don't know about war, Bonfire. No idea what they're in for. They think this is summer camp and war will be more of the same."

We returned to the medical tents, and The Major tied me up again until late afternoon. While he was examining soldiers, another senior officer came by, the Surgeon General, Carleton Jones. He walked up to me and looked me over. Then he opened my mouth, the nerve! and looked at my teeth. He was a very officious character with a snotty manner, and I didn't like him one bit.

The Major appeared. "Can I help you, Jones?" he asked, his face tight with disdain.

For the first time, I saw that the kind manner I was getting used to in The Major could completely disappear. These two men did not like each other at all.

"General Jones, to you Doctor McCrae. This must be the horse Todd gave you," he said. "Quite nice."

"Yes, and that's Major McCrae. Now, what can I do for you?" asked The Major very formally.

"Just came by to see how you were doing with the exams." Which was false. I could tell he was angling to tell him something quite unrelated to that. "I have to tell you, Major, that medicals are not supposed to have horses. You must know that."

"But I am *not* in the medical corps. *You* must know *that*. I am in the 1st Brigade Canadian Field Artillery and have not been assigned to that happy band of . . . to the medical corps. As second in command of the 1st Brigade, Canadian Field Artillery," he repeated, "I am not only allowed to have a mount, it's a requirement."

"Sir William said you were the finest physician of your generation. What *could* he have been thinking?" Jones's eyes narrowed, and he spat out the words. "A highly qualified doctor, wasting his time in the artillery." The Surgeon General stood there and seethed for a moment. "We'll be covering this ground again, Major."

Jones had referred to Sir William Osler, the famous pioneer of modern medicine and The Major's friend and mentor.

"Do excuse me, General," said The Major, "I have many men to attest yet today. Goodbye." And with that, he turned his back on the man and turned back to the examination tent.

Standing and watching in the door of the tent was a slim young captain with tattoos on his forearms, his cap at a rakish angle and a mischievous glint in his eye. I'd seen him the day I was given to The Major.

"Cosgrave! You brat. When did you sneak in here?" The two men shook hands vigorously. "You didn't witness that exchange, did you?"

"No, but I saw him heading this way and followed him over. He looked like he was on a mission. What did he say?"

"Just some tripe about medical officers not being allowed mounts. He just can't get over the fact that I've chosen the artillery over the army medical corps."

Another voice chimed in. It was the portly, bow-legged Colonel Morrison.

"This feud goes somewhat deeper than whether or not medicals get horses. It goes all the way back to South Africa and that other war. Before your time, laddy," The Colonel said to Captain Cosgrave. "And that is a very long story that I shall tell you someday over a bottle of Scotch. But not today."

The men laughed, and The Colonel wrinkled his nose. "Speaking of Boers, Major, what in the world are you smoking in that pipe? It smells like that godawful Boer tobacco."

"It's a blend called Old Chum. Quite nice actually."

"Old Barnyard more like," said The Colonel, and the men laughed, including The Major. "Say, what did you ever do with your profanity notebook? Do you still have that thing?"

The Major said nothing but shook his finger at The Colonel. All the men raised their eyebrows, their curiosity much piqued by this.

The Colonel said, "He used to keep a little notebook of the, how shall I put it? Of the more colourful expressions of the common, and I do mean common . . . um, scintillations of genius from the Canadian artilleryman in the field." The men snickered. "Some of those men of ours were amazingly inventive with their . . . barrages of blasphemy. Eh, Major?"

Captain Cosgrave let loose a guffaw, slapping his knee. "That's a good one, Colonel. Barrage of blasphemy."

The Major snorted and laughed. "I believe Mother put it on the burn pile at the farm."

"She did not, did she? There were some gems in there," said The Colonel, with pretend distress.

I liked the feeling between these men; good humour, a warm, easy friendship and respect.

"Listen, Jack, we need to assess these horses tomorrow. How's his leg?"

The Colonel walked over and looked. "Looks good, but maybe not ready for riding? What do you think?"

Jack. So that was The Major's name. Jack was much too familiar a title for me to use, but I liked the sound of it.

"I think I'll see how he is tomorrow. One more night should bring him along to where I can ride him. I'm pretty sure he'll be ready to-morrow although I'm not going to push him too hard. I'll start with him and then take a turn on the bay. Then I'll make my decision."

"Fine," said The Colonel. "I'll be at your tent at 10:00 a.m."

My stomach turned to jelly. Bonfire: Fox Hunter Extraordinaire probably had one chance and one chance only to convince these men that he was good enough for The Major. And I was still up against that demon, Thor! I resolved to do my utmost, even if I was in pain. I would not show it. Nothing was going to stop me from convincing The Major to choose me for his charger.

After another slathering of the special elixir, Dodge put me to bed in the tent-stable. I didn't sleep well with the worrying. Finally I dozed off, but not until well into the small hours.

THREE

At dawn, I awoke to the smell of rain. I listened but could not hear it. At least it hadn't started. Dodge led me out under a black and threatening sky. That would be all I would need, rain and the slippery footing it would cause.

"Too dark in here without the sun. I need to look at that leg of yours," said Dodge, and I felt his nerves too. "Let's have a look," he said, and peeled off the bandage. "Well, Bonfire. It looks good. Very good, indeed. You're as ready as you're going to be." He gave a worried look up to the sky. "Providing rain doesn't turn this into a greasy mess before you show us what you're capable of."

He patted me on my neck and ran his hand over my withers. "Best get you tacked up."

Thor was standing outside tied to a horse line. He looked as miserable as ever. Since he'd recovered from the grueling ride The Major had taken him on, some of the attitude had already returned. I looked away from him and resolved to concentrate only on the trial ahead of me.

The Major seemed one of the most reasonable humans I'd ever encountered. I would trust that he would make the right decision. As my Irish draught horse mother, Tessa would say, "Bonfire, what's for ye won't pass ye."

Dodge's voice jolted me back into the present. "Bonfire, I'm going to leave the bandage off. Once you start really moving out it would just come off anyway."

The Major came out of his tent and rubbed his hands together as he walked toward me. Then he looked up and his face became as cloudy as the dark sky above us. To his credit he said nothing, but I knew by his expression that he was anxious about it.

Dodge brushed me and threw the old cavalry saddle onto my back. The Major had kept his saddle from South African days and this was a source of amusement for the men. They thought it strange that he preferred the old thing instead of the modern saddles all the officers had been issued. Well, it might have been old, but it was comfortable and fit the two of us perfectly.

The Major walked around me and then knelt beside my leg.

"This looks remarkable. First class. It's almost healed." He stood. "I'm going to ride him first, hopefully before the rain. I want him ready to go as soon as The Colonel gets here," he studied his pocket watch, "in . . . about . . . two minutes. Being the punctual character that he is."

He hardly had the words out when we heard a trotting horse and Colonel Morrison and his great grey charger, King, came up the road. King was a regal sort of animal, dapple grey and no-nonsense, like The Colonel. They were perfectly suited, both commanding the respect of both man and beast. The Colonel didn't dismount.

"C'mon, Jack, let's go. I thought we'd go round the track that circles the entire camp. It's a good five miles, and there are a few bush jumps laid out for us. I had my man do it last night, with Lex and Cosgrave's assistance. Then we'll do Thor after lunch."

The Colonel looked down at my leg from his perch aboard King.

"What was it you said about some magic horse elixir? Something must have worked very well indeed. You can hardly tell he was hurt. At least not from up here anyway."

Dodge put on my bridle and The Major mounted. I noticed immediately how soft his hands were. There was no reefing or jerking on my mouth like some of those rough fox-hunt riders, excluding Marjory Todd of course. She was a master. The Major, what a blessing! I'd imagined he'd be gentle that way, but one never knows. I felt him inhale deeply and then give his shoulders a shake to calm his nerves.

He ran both hands down the sides of my neck and whispered, "Ready, Bonfire?" And then to The Colonel, "Let's go."

As we walked down the path side by side toward the track where my trial was to take place, I inhaled deeply the scent of pine from the trees that encircled the camp. Divine. We walked toward Thor, tied to the horse line, and he didn't move a muscle but couldn't help pinning his ears back as we passed.

The Major and The Colonel noticed that and shared a look.

Colonel Morrison said only one word, "Glue," and the two men laughed out loud. These men were close friends, probably had been since that South African war. It was pure fun to be in their company.

We turned onto the track and The Colonel said, "Let's go."

The Major gently squeezed my sides with his legs. Aaah, another good habit. He was not a kicker. I broke into a smooth trot and made a concerted effort not to show favour to my injured leg in any way.

25

John "Jack" McCrae, Valcartier, 17 September, 1914

King and I matched each other well, stride for stride. The two men looked at each other, and The Major nodded and said, "Lovely and smooth."

We trotted for a half mile and then changed to a canter. I could see a pile of brush ahead, the first jump. My leg still felt bruised, but I resolved to ignore it. Colonel Morrison and King sped up and cleared the jump first, then the Major and I followed. I do love to jump, and I flew over it with more than a couple of feet to spare. My landing was smooth. The Colonel had stopped and turned to face us as we rode up.

And that's when I heard yet another name for The Major.

"Wipe that grin off your face, McCrae," said The Colonel. The Major just shook his head, all smiles.

The world would eventually know The Major as John McCrae, but to all the humans who knew him well and loved him, he would always be known as Jack.

"He is marvelous. Just marvelous!" said The Major. "I knew he would be, if we could just get him over the injury."

Colonel Morrison turned King, and off we went at a comfortable canter. We completely circled the camp. The eleven remaining jumps were a cakewalk for me, being used to four- and five-foot-high stone walls, ditches and the like. Adrenalin now completely numbed any pain in my leg, and I felt more than thrilled to be carrying this kind officer. It was an honour.

Toward the very end, when we'd almost come full circle, The Major squeezed my sides and cued me for a gallop. King and I ran for another quarter mile, and I had the edge in speed. Right at the end there was a pen with a five-foot fence. The Major pointed me at it, and we galloped toward it. Okay, I thought, this will be a breeze.

But the ground was uneven, and I almost stumbled. I regained my balance with a few feet to go. The Major crouched up over my neck and gave me my head, and I flew over that fence with the best form I could muster.

A surprised man working at the back of the pen hurriedly stepped to one side and then applauded. "Well done, Major."

The Major doffed his cap and bowed like a competitor in the show ring. The Colonel had a laugh on the other side of the fence with King. He slapped King on his neck.

"Old King, here, is capable, but I'm getting too old for it, I'm afraid. Good show there, Jack. No contest? Is Thor out of the running?"

"No contest," said The Major. "Bonfire? We're partners and that's that."

The man in the pen opened the gate so we could come back out, and I felt like I was walking on air. I admit I was breathing hard after standing around for so long without exercise, but I knew it wouldn't be long before I recovered my wind and fitness.

"How about a celebratory lunch, Colonel?" asked The Major. "I believe Dodge has made tea and sandwiches."

"Splendid," said Colonel Morrison. He admired me as we walked. "He really is a beauty, too," he said. Of course I did know that, but it still caused me to blush.

We came by Thor again, and I avoided looking at him as we passed. The two men made no comment either. I felt a little sorry for the surly bay fellow. I don't know why. He probably had some good reason for his bad temper, but we would not likely ever know the why of it.

When we got back to my stall, The Major dismounted, groaning in pain, and Dodge took my reins.

"A good long walk for the Chestnut Gentleman, Dodge. Until he's dry, and then water and a scoop of oats."

The Chestnut Gentleman. Oh, my. I loved it. I felt very proud to have such a man give me such a title.

"And then I need you to prepare me a hot bath if I'm to be able to walk tomorrow at all. Good Lord! Fourteen years of doctoring have left me very rusty in the riding department. By the way, Dodge," said The Major, "that elixir, is there any sort of a label on it?"

"Actually there is a small label that says something in a foreign language, sir. I'm afraid I don't read French or anything. Foreign languages wasn't top of our list in Portsmouth, Major."

"Not to worry. There are other skills, Dodge, like blacksmithing, which you do very well indeed. But go and get me that bottle, will you?" The Major took my reins again.

Dodge came back with the honey-coloured oil and handed the bottle to The Major. The Colonel looked on curiously. The Major squinted at the label and burst into laughter.

"Hmm, made in India." The Major looked up. "Your old Sergeant Major Fraser served with the British Army in India, correct?"

"Correct, sir," said Dodge, smartly.

"It says Palma Christi," The Major said, and laughed again. "Palma Christi."

"Which is the Latin name for castor oil," said Colonel Morrison with a laugh. "The mysterious and magical elixir is our old friend, castor oil."

Dodge turned beet-red and said, "Hmmph," with a cranky expression.

I had the impression that he felt a little cheated by his old Sergeant Major, now deceased, who'd given him the liniment and billed it as a magical concoction of his own creation. It was as if the elder sergeant had played a trick on him.

"But what do the words mean, sir, Palma Christi?" Dodge asked.

The Major and The Colonel fell briefly into a thoughtful silence.

"In English it means the palm, or the hand, of Christ," said The Major.

All I knew is that I was blessed to be with The Major and these men.

* * *

Artillery column, Valcartier, Quebec 1914

By October, 1914, Camp Valcartier, Quebec, had readied itself to send the first wave of soldiers and horses across the ocean, and that meant us.

The last time I saw Thor before leaving for our ship, he was one of six horses pulling a heavy field gun under the barking orders of a burly, red-faced driver. He didn't see me, and I didn't envy the poor soul. He had his head down as he struggled across a muddy, humpy-bumpy field, pulling for all he was worth. I would see him again, but it would not be until the Salisbury Plain.

PART TWO

TO ENGLAND

FOUR

"You men!" bellowed Colonel Morrison.

I nearly jumped out of my skin because he was sitting on King right beside The Major and me.

"You there! Stop dithering around there and form up." The Colonel huffed and turned to The Major. "It's like herding bloody cats, I swear. Captain Cosgrave, get those men and wagons into formation."

Captain Cosgrave trotted his horse toward the rear, where there was a tangle of wagons, some criss-crossed. Some horses reared in harness, and red-faced drivers tried to gain control of their teams.

The Major turned me around to face the gathering soldiers and spoke to young Lex, who was near the front.

"Lieutenant Helmer, go down and check on the guns. I don't want to hear of any damage. We can't afford it."

"Yes, sir," said Lex smartly, and off he rode on a handsome, bay thoroughbred gelding with a crooked white blaze down its face and over one nostril. Lex was a nice boy, and I was relieved that he had not gotten stuck with Thor. That cantankerous animal was now consigned to hauling guns and would never be anyone's mount again.

The Major turned me to face forward again. We stood at the head of the artillery column and prepared to move out. The Major seemed excited and chuckled under his breath. As he puffed on his pipe, he patted my neck, and the sweet tobacco smoke swirled around my head. I liked the smell of it. The atmosphere was electric as men, horses, mules, field guns and wagons in great numbers got organized and ready to march to Quebec City and the ship that would take us down the great Saint Lawrence River and eventually "across the pond," to England.

The mood was entirely one of excitement—a great adventure was about to unfold. Horses are brilliant at detecting the emotional states of their riders. Some, whose names I will not mention, have even taken ruthless advantage of the fearful rider. Not I, of course, but it's easy to do. On this day I could sense some fear and anxiety, but overall, the feeling was that of great anticipation. None of us knew how dramatically that positive expectation would be shattered in the months and years to come.

On the quay in Quebec City, we horses looked at one another. There was no comfort or reassurance to be found. Not one of us had ever walked up a plank onto an oddly shaped building that floated on the water. The only thing I could do was take my confidence from The Major, who, with Colonel Morrison, had done this exact thing fourteen years earlier with horses and an artillery brigade, except the destination had been Johannesburg, South Africa. The Major was as calm as anything as he led me up the plank, followed by Dodge. King was behind us being led by Colonel Morrison's man, but we were soon separated. Once we were below decks, King and I called to each other a couple of times, but he sounded far away, perhaps the opposite side of the hold.

So there I was in a tiny box stall in the bottom of a ship with two mules on one side and a cayuse from Alberta on the other! The mules were a matched pair, at least colour—dark bay—and size-wise, and their handler, Jock Oliphant from Medicine Hat, seemed to have a very high regard for them. He fussed over them at regular intervals. Magnus was beside me and Monty, which I came to discover was short for Montague, was beside him. Such lofty names for such lowly beasts, I thought.

Magnus was shorter than me, but what he lacked in stature he made up for in attitude. He had this quiet, imperious way of looking "down" at me that made me feel self-conscious, like a small colt again. Me, Bonfire! It was irritating but inescapable. Monty, on the other hand, was a goofball, plain and simple. On his own he would have been completely useless, but Magnus kept him in line, and

1st Brigade CFA being loaded on *S.S. Saxonia*

Monty's strong point was that he was extremely powerful. I heard Jock tell another groom that on his own, Monty would only turn left. Someone had gotten him in the habit, as a youngster, of leaving out the farm gate and turning left to town. Well, that was that. To get him to turn right ever after was a tremendous battle. A classic illustration of mules' renowned stubborn and, I don't mind saying, stupid streak. But when the more sensible Magnus was alongside him, Monty would do whatever he did.

With a frightful roaring of engines and a shouting of men, our ship, *Saxonia*, lurched away from the quay in Quebec City and began the slow, swishing journey down the St. Lawrence River to the Atlantic Ocean. It was October 3, 1914. On board our ship were 632 horses and mules, The Major, and the entire 1st Brigade Canadian Field Artillery and all their men and equipment.

The Major insisted that Dodge check on my well-being as often as possible. The fact was, The Major himself came down at least once a day and quite often with treats for me: biscuits, apples, raspberries and other delights. I would nicker a greeting as soon as I saw him; a deep, throaty sort of equine purr, only shorter, which The Major called a whicker. He would smile when he heard it.

"Bonfire, you've got the best whicker of any horse I've ever known."

Young Lex Helmer came down too. After he'd checked on his own horse, he'd pay me a visit as well. I can't swear to it, but I think the inscrutable Magnus rolled his eyes at this. Well, it was one thing to fuss over mules, but quite another to fuss over the Chestnut Gentleman!

The cayuse to my right was a short, stout, black-and-white paint with a white face and two spooky-looking blue eyes. Ghost kept to himself except when our meagre two flakes of hay were delivered, twice a day. Then he'd pin back his ears and make a show of challenging me for it, which was silly because we each had our own manger. I learned to ignore him.

We could hear the strains of a pipe band playing on the decks above as we glided down the river. Every now and then cheers would erupt from the men above that would be answered by throngs of onlookers lining the river banks. The Canadian anthem, "The Maple Leaf Forever," was played and sung repeatedly with great gusto. It all seemed very celebratory. I wondered why the celebrations did not make me feel as happy as they should have?

It soon became evident there was a shortage of handlers on the *Saxonia*, and poor Dodge had to care for about a dozen of us. I resented having to share him with other horses, but there was no choice in the matter. He did his best to attend to me the way The Major had instructed him and apologized to me often for his long absences. He mucked us all out as well as he could, and I was afraid he was being overtaxed in the process. He would appear puffing, flushed and perspiring as he tried to stay ahead of the manure.

"Sorry, Master Bonfire. It's an awful situation, it is. Too many horses and not enough men."

What can I say? It's simply a bare fact of us horses. Eating hay creates manure and drinking water creates urine. As time passed, the stench of sweat, manure and the smell of ammonia (from the urine), became overpowering and made our eyes water.

The Major was as kind as ever to me on his visits, but as he came and went, I'd hear him grumble under his breath, "This is a disgrace," and, "Good Lord, what a smell."

Well, it was a sorry situation for man and beast when we reached Gaspé Harbour. Just as the soldiers had to form up before we all marched from Valcartier to Quebec City, the thirty-three ships of the Canadian Expeditionary Force had to form up before entering the massive Gulf of St. Lawrence. The ventilation below decks was non-existent. Add to that autumn heat and stillness as we waited for all the ships to arrive, and it was quite intolerable. In all, the thirty-three ships contained upwards of eight thousand horses!

At some point while we waited, a small, noisy launch came by and a loud man aboard it hollered up to the men above on the decks.

"Soldiers! As you embark upon this sacred quest, the eyes of Canada and indeed the world are upon you. You will be brave and you will be victorious. You will be as fine a body of men as has ever faced a foe. You are the pride of this great nation, and God is with you!"

I knew that voice. It was that puffed up minister, formerly of the militia but now, Minister of War, Sam Hughes, that I had seen at Valcartier inspecting the chaplains. He seemed a windy character, and most soldiers didn't take him seriously. Peals of laughter could be heard above as his launch motored away.

Finally we began to move into the yawning Gulf of St. Lawrence toward the Atlantic Ocean. Our ships formed up into three columns of eleven escorted by six British war ships, one at the front and back of each column. The further we travelled out, the more the welcome sea air came down to us below decks and blew the stuffiness out of our quarters. What a relief.

Dodge appeared suddenly beside me. "We're off, Master Bonfire." He patted me vigorously on the withers. "Only twenty-five hundred miles to go, and I'll get to see me old England for the first time in a dozen years."

Twenty-five hundred miles? Across water? Good grief.

I must say, Bonfire, Fox Hunter Extraordinaire, was bored beyond belief just standing in a tiny stall with no exercise, not even a walk. It was the most tedious experience of my life. We horses can certainly sleep on our feet, and often do. But how I missed a good lie-down in the sun, a roll in the dirt or a gallop and a good buck. I sorely missed my stall at home on Doctor Todd's farm–a large, classy affair with brass fittings and luxurious piles of soft, clean, yellow straw. There was even a brass plate above my stall door with "Bonfire" engraved on it. Plus, I had to contend with Magnus the mule looking haughtily down his nose at me like I was a novice and he knew things I didn't. And worse, it was probably true. I was a sporting horse amidst a herd of cavalry and work horses. Oh, and let us not forget the mules.

But nothing could dampen the legendary Bonfire appetite, even as our ship gently rolled over the waves. Food was the only thing I had to look forward to to break the monotony. The cayuse on my left went right off his food. He just picked at it a little without enthusiasm. Magnus and Monty seemed not to care one way or another, about anything. Their handler was another matter. Even though I heard other handlers say we were being blessed with a smooth crossing, Jock threw up into a bucket regularly for the next twelve days that our crossing took. The poor fellow, already fair-skinned, was thin and as white as the chalk sea-cliffs by the time we approached the shores of England.

FIVE

We'd been blessed with a smooth crossing for almost the whole twelve days, but our luck was about to change with terrible effect. A storm blew up over the waters with gale-force winds. Our big ships were tossed about like so many toys in a turbulent tub. We horses and mules banged our heads and smashed against our stalls and into each other. Some horses fell and scrambled to their feet again. I tried to calm myself with hopes of a visit from The Major, but I learned that he was run off his feet attending to injuries of both soldiers and horses. Thankfully, we only had a short journey in the storm before arriving at Plymouth, and the injuries were minor.

We then began the complicated, time-consuming, chaotic chore of disembarking thirty thousand men and nearly eight thousand horses. We were all to be loaded onto trains and taken to the training ground on Salisbury Plain. Our brigade's disembarkation wasn't as confusing as the others' since we had our own ship and no one other than the 1st Brigade Canadian Field Artillery was on it.

As we left our ships, after much waiting, we received a rousing welcome from the English people. Hundreds of well-wishers shouted and cheered and showered our soldiers with kisses and hugs, cigarettes and candies. The Major and Dodge had the good sense to give their peppermints to me. Yum. It took nine days for all of us, the entire Canadian Expeditionary Force, to come ashore and get aboard our trains.

On the quay, a tough-looking, battle-scarred English sergeant saluted and spoke to The Major and Captain Cosgrave as they walked ahead of Dodge and me. "Sirs," he nodded, "it's a good job you Canucks, er . . . you Canadians have brought more horses. We're going through an awful whack of them in France."

My ears perked up anxiously. What did he mean? Going through horses?

As Dodge led me by an enthusiastic group of civilians, an elderly woman in a bonnet with silver curls framing her face spoke loudly. "I say, I thought there would be more Red Indians with them."

Dodge snorted and muttered, "There's quite a few, and they're in uniform like everyone else. Did she think they'd be in buckskins and beads? Hmph."

The Major wanted to ride to his lodgings and not bother with the train at all, but Colonel Morrison convinced him otherwise. How I would have loved to stretch out and travel a few miles on foot. It was not to be. Back onto a cramped train we went, just like the one I had taken from Doctor Todd's farm to Valcartier. At least I was with King again, and happy to be with a friend.

***

On a wide-open and wind-swept corner of the rolling Salisbury Plain, the brigade moved into another sea of white bell tents at West Down North Camp, much like the ones at Camp Valcartier. This was the only similarity. The balmy Indian summer of Valcartier gave way to one of the worst English winters in memory. Out of a hundred and twenty-three days, it rained for eighty-nine of them. The Major made a sort of lean-to shelter for me near his bell tent out of scrounged canvas and wood. But the vast majority of horses and mules had no shelter at all. Not a single stick for protection from the weather.

The soldiers were forbidden to chop down any trees near the camp. There was also a standing order on Salisbury Plain: 'No Picketing of Horses in the Trees.' We had no idea why these rules were in force. They seemed arbitrary. In the absence of any materials that could be used for horse shelters, at least the trees would have offered some protection from the lashing rain and icy winds.

The Major and I rode out to Bustard Camp one day and passed the lines of our own artillery horses. They were tied, and stood soaking wet in the wind-battered open. There was Thor, shivering in the middle of them, that unmistakable sliver of a crescent moon on his face. The whole line had their backs to the wind, ears back and heads down. Pure misery. Magnus and Monty stoically anchored one end of a line. Thor raised his head slightly as we passed, but I'm not sure his dull eyes showed any recognition.

Like trench foot, a dreadful condition similar to frostbite that soldiers would experience in the months to come as a result of standing in trenches full of water and mud, horses on the Salisbury Plain were stricken with their own version–hoof-rot, or more correctly, gangrenous dermatitis. It was as awful as it sounds.

The Major and I tried to ride out every day, but some days were just too awful for training and drilling of men, or even riding, and nothing at all could be done. In fact, The Major hardly got to do any artillery drills or duties at all at first, due to the sickness that the weather fostered. He spent most of his days examining soldiers one after another on sick parade. Everything in the military seemed to be called a parade: sick parade, church parade. He said most cases on sick parade were genuine too. Not many malingerers, which were soldiers who

45

only pretended to be sick, to get out of work or drilling. Before the military, the only parades I had seen were fun and festive ones.

One bone-chilling November day as we toured the camp a loud voice shouted, "McCrae. Major McCrae!" The Major turned to look and so did I. There was a stout, balding man, a civilian, with glasses and a thick black moustache. His black umbrella was threatening to turn inside-out in the wind. I could feel The Major's excitement run through him into me. He fairly leapt to the ground in dismount and dragged me to the man by my reins as they both extended their arms and shook hands vigourously.

"Rudyard Kipling! Mr. Kipling, how are you, sir?"

"I am very well. It's good to see you." Kipling pointedly looked up at the black sky. "Can you Canadians not place yourselves some-where with a more moderate climate?" The two men laughed. "I be-lieve last time we met it was in the blazing heat of South Africa."

"Yes, it was," said The Major.

"Well, that was quite a different war. My boy Jack is in this one." He swelled up with pride as he declared, "He's in the Irish Guards."

"You don't say," said The Major. "Congratulations. You must be very proud."

"Yes, I am. He's in France and off to the front as we speak."

"We shall pray for his safe return, then."

Kipling looked at his pocket watch as a car pulled up for him. "I have to dash, but I'll be back for lunch tomorrow. We'll catch up. I hear you're soldiering and doctoring, too, this time. Is that right?"

"Mainly doctoring at the moment, today anyway, but I'll serve wher-ever the call is loudest. And right now, this appalling weather is keep-ing me busy treating soldiers with colds, pneumonia, flu, bronchitis."

"I shouldn't wonder. Say, Colonel Morrison tells me you're quite the poet too. Man of many talents. I'd love to read some of your pieces sometime."

The Major instantly blushed; something I hadn't seen before.

"Ah, well . . . I . . . I dabble a little. Certainly nothing of the calibre of your works, sir."

"Now now," said Kipling, wagging his finger, "you're being modest. Well, it's good to see you again, Major, and we'll talk over lunch."

As the two men shook hands again, I realized a small crowd of soldiers had gathered and were watching and whispering. This Kipling, I later found out, was the famous writer of the Todd children's favourite collection of stories, *The Jungle Book*. I found it strange, the people that war brought together. I also found it strange that he was so happy about his boy being "off to the front." Humans befuddled me sometimes.

Canadian soldiers "mudlarking" on Salisbury Plain, England 1914

Kipling climbed into the car and drove off with a breezy wave as the sky opened up again. The Major mounted and we carried on to Bustard Camp. The Major wanted to check on the wooden huts that were being built for the soldiers.

The soldiers were actually in amazingly good form and spirits, given the conditions. Other than the irritation of lice, or vermin, as The Major referred to them, the men's suffering could not be compared to that of the horses. They seemed to be able to joke about their lot, and some of the soldiers even composed poems and songs about the conditions. One particular poem gave The Major a good laugh. How I loved to hear that deep, full-throated laugh. It always warmed my insides. Captain Cosgrave recited it one day after lunch. First, he straightened his cap from its usual rakish angle. Then, he rested his hand on an old table outside the officers' mess tent, like an opera singer at a grand piano. With great formality and grand hand gestures he cleared his throat and began.

"On Salisbury Plain. / On Salisbury Plain, under gloomy skies, the mud doth lie." At this point he stopped and explained, "Dotthh," he said, exhaling loudly through his teeth, and then wiping his mouth with his handkerchief, "Dotthh, is English for does." The men laughed as he began again. Someone from the back shouted, "Get on with it!" More laughter.

"On Salisbury Plain, under gloomy skies, the mud doth lie. / Up to our knees, even up to our thighs, the mud doth lie. / Mud in our hair, even mud in our eyes. / Mud in our snake and pygmy pies . . . ahem ahem, " He coughed and cleared his throat. "Do pardon me. / Mud in our steak and kidney pies, / Mud under dirty, rotten, gloomy skies, / On Salisbury Plain."

* * *

At Bustard Camp, The Major checked on the progress of the men's huts, but just as important to him, was there any sign of shelters being built for the horses yet? No. Not one sign that we could see. We headed back to camp, and I could feel The Major's disappointment.

Back in our camp, The Major's mood brightened again. We were greeted by a beautiful, tiger-striped, grey cat that The Major had christened Miss Kitty. If the weather was fair at all, she would come outside and wind herself around my legs. And if I put my muzzle down to her, she would stand right up on her hind legs and rub her face against my nose, which made me sneeze and The Major laugh. But if even one raindrop came down, she would dive into The Major's tent and snuggle into his bed. He told Dodge he didn't want to get too attached to her because we would be leaving soon and then what would become of her?

Dodge said to me, "Master Bonfire, it's too late. He just dotes on Miss Kitty already. The Major is an old softie for the creatures. But you would know that," he said, and I certainly did.

* * *

People were great letter writers in those days, and The Major was one of the most diligent. He wrote letters daily to family and friends, and received them from his mother, brother Tom–also a doctor–and his sister Geills. Geills was married with children and lived in Winnipeg. She sent him a book by his friend from Montreal, Stephen Leacock. It was funny to hear him burst into laughter from inside his tent every so often as he read it.

The Major and Stephen Leacock had belonged to an informal club in Montreal called The Pen and Pencil Club, whereby they would meet every two weeks and read their writings: poetry, short stories, essays and so on. Colonel Morrison said, "The Pen and Pencil Club was code for The Scotch Drinking Club," which I didn't quite understand. The Major always chuckled when he said it though.

He was writing at a small table outside his tent when Lex came by to ask him about horse shelter progress. After The Major had updated him on the not-so-good news, the young lieutenant asked with impatience, "When are we going over to France, Major? It will all be finished before we get there and we'll miss the whole show. They say it will be over by Christmas. "

"And that is a stupid statement to make. We'll get over soon enough, Lex. We haven't even had proper drills and training here yet because of this . . .this . . ."

The Major spread his arms out, and we all looked at the morass in front of us.

"I say we learn by doing," Lex persisted. "No better teacher than experience, don't you agree, Major?"

"In some things, son. But not in artillery fighting. War is serious business. The better the training, the more effective we are and the more likely we'll be to come through."

I wondered what he meant, come through. Come through what? I didn't like the sound of that.

SIX

The weather went from terrible to disastrous. Endless, relentless rain and raging winds were getting on The Major's nerves. Except for the persistent dampness, he was reasonably comfortable in his tent thanks to long underwear, good wool blankets and a wool nightcap. But any comfort he might have felt gave way to anxiety as he was wracked with worry and losing sleep over the deteriorating condition of the horses. I, too, felt quite well, due to The Major and Dodge's good care of me, but many other horses were starting to fail.

On Salisbury Plain, the hard chalk base beneath the thin layer of soil did not absorb the water, so it sat on the surface in massive, mucky pools. If the sky did clear at all, the air would be damp with a biting cold, accompanied always by wind. On a day without rain, everything would usually be covered with hoarfrost that would just stay all day, with no sun strong enough to burn it off. The icy winds seemed to go right into our bones. No progress was being made on the horse-shelter front, and The Major's disappointment was evolving into a simmering anger. The Colonel and The Major repeatedly requested materials for horse shelters from HQ (headquarters), and were only met with an infuriating silence.

The Colonel, The Major and the brigade's officers at least got respite a few times in the nearby village of Devizes. My favourite stable was at The Bear Inn, our brigade's officers' mess. Staying there was a gift for us horses, too. We got to sleep in lovely, DRY, straw-filled stalls in the barns behind the inn for a night or two.

The other place in Devizes was a cozy hotel called The Ark. One night we stayed there with Captain Cosgrave and General Edwin Alderson, the English general in charge of all of the Canadians. He was a senior career soldier who had fought in South Africa, too, and many battles even before that. In the weeks to come, he would have high praise for us Canadians. In too short of a time though, it was out of our comfy lodgings and back to cold, wet, West Down North Camp.

The night of December 2 there was a terrific storm, even worse than the usual awful weather. The gale-force winds seemed to pull and blow from every direction and the rain was torrential. Tents blew down and my lean-to shelter simply blew away. The Major, Dodge, Lex, Captain Cosgrave and several soldiers from the brigade went against the rules. They led about two dozen of us horses, in pairs, into the trees for protection from the battering. It was scary as they led us in. Branches noisily whipped every which way and some even broke off and landed on us. Wild shadows danced across the trees and us, too. I tried to be calm and an example to the others, some of whom were panicking. As ever, I took my cue from The Major, who was calm but determined.

We were hardly picketed and settled into the wood when two British officers from HQ appeared in the dark. One was a colonel with a shock of white hair, a white handlebar moustache and chilling, pale-grey eyes. He spoke very rudely to The Major.

"You, there! McCrae, isn't it? Listen here, McCrae, what part of, 'No Picketing of Horses in the Woods Round Salisbury Plain' do you not understand? Get those blasted horses out of the trees at once!"

Even in this gale, the HQ staff refused to bend the rules about tying up horses in the forest. The Major, Dodge, Cosgrave and Lex untied us all and led us back into the howling gale again.

Captain Cosgrave, never one to stick too closely to protocol, asked the colonel, "What is the reason for this rule? Can an exception not be made? These horses are failing without shelter and with every day of this damnable weather."

When The Major found out the reason, his face turned scarlet and his eyes filled with tears of frustration and anger. I'd never seen him in such a state and hoped never to see him like that again. The colonel ignored Cosgrave's question and stormed away. But his adjutant, a young captain, apologetically told him the woods needed to be protected as habitat for foxes because of the sport of fox hunting!

Fox hunting on Salisbury Plain was a higher priority than the welfare of soldiers and their horses. For the first time in my life, I, Bonfire, Fox Hunter Extraordinaire, felt ashamed of my sport and disgusted with the humans who participated in it.

The next morning, Lex Helmer's beautiful bay gelding was found lying dead in the lines. He was a fine horse, but a thin-skinned, scantly coated thoroughbred and just not able for these awful conditions. He had died of exposure in the night.

Even oats, a little extra fuel for us horses, would have helped. But there were no oats due to our hosts' lack of interest in making any available to us.

This storm and its aftermath was the last straw. Getting nowhere with requests for horse shelters, The Colonel and The Major had been inquiring about renting a large farm for the brigade and its horses. New Copse Farm was two miles northwest of the present camp at West Down. At last they were allowed to make this arrangement, and on December 8, two hundred horses in the worst shape were moved to

New Copse Farm, where they could finally get out of the elements and begin to recover. The Staff at HQ also relaxed the rule about picketing horses in the trees. We could now be kept in the wood.

Sadly, it was too late for the black and white cayuse. He was tough, but he was used to the dry lands and bald prairies of southeastern Alberta. His hooves had rotted beyond recovery from standing in muck for too long, and he had to be put down. No foot, no horse.

New Copse Farm was heaven for all of us horses and men after our windswept camp. Magnus and Monty both had cases of ringworm, but that was easy to treat. They were otherwise in good health, although they had to be kept away from all of us horses The men had to be careful around them, too, until it was healed up. Thor was among the worst cases of exposure after weeks of standing in cold, rain and wind. He had to be treated with extra care and food until he recovered. He was a hide-draped skeleton, and any trace of his former feistiness was nowhere in evidence. I felt genuinely sorry for him.

Shortly after our arrival at New Copse Farm, wooden huts were completed for most of the men. They left their bell tents for what were supposed to be more comfortable barracks. Well, they should have remained in the tents. Although cold and damp, the tents were at least well ventilated, unlike the warm huts, which had tiny windows and forced the men into close quarters.

The men, upon leaving the warm huts, would get chilled to the bone. This and the poor ventilation led to more illness with fatal consequences. In January of 1915, a meningitis outbreak swept through the huts and left twenty-seven soldiers and a chaplain dead.

Our lodging at New Copse Farm turned out to be short-lived. One thing I was learning about the military was that circumstances changed continually and, as often as not, abruptly. We horses, being such creatures of habit, found this very disconcerting at first, but we gradually became as hardened to it as the soldiers. The only sure thing in the military, I learned, was that nothing was for sure!

The weather improved a little during our last days at the farm. Several times The Major and I rode out with The Colonel and King to watch our batteries drill; gunners set fuses, registered and fired on targets. Our drivers cleaned harnesses and practised harnessing teams quickly and driving limbers (part of a gun carriage), and guns to certain points on the plain.

Captain Cosgrave, General Alderson and John McCrae on Bonfire at The Ark, Devizes, England 1915

The firing of the big artillery guns was a new thing for me and something I had to work hard at getting used to. The sheer loudness of the explosions made every nerve in my body jangle and actually hurt my ears. I just wanted to run in the opposite direction, but The Major was calm, and he forced me to stand. There was nothing to do but tolerate it. But it was something I would always dislike. Also, aeroplanes flew around overhead. Good grief. Like giant but noisy birds they were, and just another thing we had to learn to abide. So much newness and change. There just was no point of reference for most of what we were being exposed to on a daily basis.

Other than observing and inspecting drill, The Major spent most of our last days on Salisbury Plain inoculating hundreds of soldiers against typhoid fever. A few men refused to take the shot and were sent home as a result. He told Dodge they probably had "cold feet" and thought it better to find that out now, rather than once we were into the war.

With the improved weather in the last days, The Colonel was happy. The Major was happy too, to be involved in artillery drill and something other than his arduous medical duties at last.

Our brigade was broken up again briefly and then all of it reunited loosely in and around the village of Devizes. And that was where we stayed for the next short while until our departure for France . . . and for war.

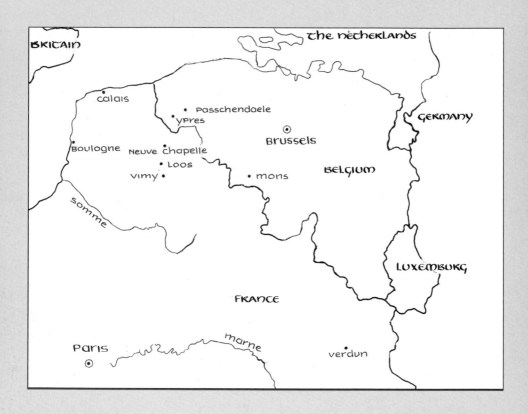

PART THREE

TO FRANCE

SEVEN

The Major began to rush about, organizing and reorganizing his kit which was in two piles on the ground in front of the barn at the back of The Bear Inn in Devizes. Back and forth he went, talking quietly to himself, "I'll need that," and "won't need that," and "that thing is useless." In the last case, he referred to Minister Hughes's secretary's invention: the MacAdams Shovel. This was an entrenching tool with a hole in it that, supposedly could be used to dig but also to fire a gun through. The Major held it up and looked at Dodge through the off-centre, teardrop-shaped hole.

"What do you think, Dodge?" Dodge wrinkled his nose. "Nothing better than a shovel with a hole in the middle of it, don't you think?" The Major laughed but Dodge did not.

"Someone's making money off that useless article," said Dodge with disgust.

"You are absolutely right, and I'm pretty sure I know who it is, but I shall keep that to myself."

Another voice piped up. Captain Cosgrave appeared suddenly, leaned against my neck and twiddled my mane as Dodge brushed my back and rump.

"Would it be the selfsame purveyors of the Ross rifle, do you think?" Cosgrave asked, with an impish glint in his eye.

"Cosgrave!" The Major looked up from his medical bag. "You rascal." Both men laughed. "And do not disparage the Ross yet. It will be proven on the battlefield. Where's The Colonel?"

"He's gone to HQ for last minute orders. He was packed and ready last night."

A small, curly-haired private appeared with a bag full of mail.

"Mail call, Major McCrae." He handed The Major several letters. There was nothing for Dodge.

"Thank you, Private. I suppose we will be in France the next time we get mail."

The Major opened a letter while Cosgrave sat on a bench against the barn wall and lit a cigarette. The Major began to read and then laughed out loud.

"It's from Mother. She asks, 'How are the McCrae boys?' " He laughed again, walked over to me and gave my forehead a scratch. "How do you like that, Bonfire? We are now The McCrae Boys."

"Seems fitting to me," said Cosgrave with a grin.

Just then Colonel Morrison rode up on King and dismounted. He handed King's reins to Dodge as his man was away, attending to other duties.

"Right, you men. Organize yourselves and get around front for an official photograph of the Officers of the First Brigade, CFA." He looked at his pocket watch. "The photographer will be here in ten minutes."

John McCrae, btm lt., Col. Morrison, btm ctr, Capt. Cosgrave, btm 3rd rt,
Lex Helmer, top 5th lt, at The Bear Hotel, Devizes, England, 1915

I could sense excitement emanating from The Colonel, overlain by determination and discipline. But his enthusiasm was evident all the same.

For a hastily organized photograph session, they were a smart looking group of men as they stood on the front steps of The Bear Inn. A small but starchy Colonel Morrison, in the middle, reminded me of a feisty little Bantam rooster Doctor Todd had when I was a colt. As soon as the photo was snapped, everyone scattered and shifted into high gear, and we prepared to move out for our ship.

Again, like our trip from Portsmouth to Salisbury Plain, there was no marching or riding as time was short. We were packed onto trains again and headed southwest for the coast. This time, King and I had luxurious adjoining box stalls, full of clean bedding. It was heaven, for a few hours anyway.

* * *

Led by Dodge, I walked up the plank onto the *SS African Prince* without a bother. It was February 9, 1915. I felt I was getting to be an old hand at this sailing business. Our trip was to be short, only a couple of days long, around to the Bay of Biscay to the port of St. Nazaire, France, on the bottom of the Brittany coast.

Other horses were in various states of fitness after the ordeal on Salisbury Plain. Most of the serious cases, who had not been put out of their misery, had somewhat recovered but still had a ways to go. I saw Thor with the other gun- and limber-pulling horses and he was still thin, but his coat was almost back to its slick, dark-bay sheen. Magnus and Monty were perfectly well. Mules are tough creatures. Lex Helmer had gotten a new horse after his first one had died, another bright-red chestnut like me. Not quite as good-looking as myself, I don't mind saying–bit of a Roman nose, and the only white at all was a short, left-hind sock. Still, he was a steady, sensible horse, and there's good value in that.

A strong wind blew as we set off. It was said the ship's usual run was around Cape Horn at the bottom of Africa, so she was well suited to nasty weather. This offered some comfort. On the other hand, we had no British war cruisers escorting us this time, like we did sailing across from Canada. Everyone hoped we'd see no sign of German submarines. The weather was terrible all night. Men were seasick and horses badly knocked about. The Major came to visit once, but it was less dangerous if everyone stayed put. Luckily, by morning, the sea had calmed considerably and everyone was very glad of it.

We sighted land on the eleventh, and by the next morning, after a quiet night on board, we were ready to disembark. Back on trains we went, eight horses and two men to a car. It was quite comfortable this time, and our rations were excellent–good hay and oats too. After the great oat famine, as I like to call it, on Salisbury Plain, we horses were all deliriously happy about this. It took two more days to get to our first billets. The train stopped at intervals, and we were led off for a stretch and a drink of water. The Major himself took me for water once, which was nice, and he also gave me treats, of course; this time it was sugar lumps and half an apple. Yesss.

Just before we got to Steenwerck, where we were to detrain for good, an excitable gelding beside me was frightened by a pigeon that flew into our train car and out again. So, what did the scatterbrain do? Lashed out sideways with a back hoof and kicked me a good one in the right hind leg. It really smarted, and soon began to throb with pain. By the time Dodge came and took me out for The Major to ride to our billet, it was bloody and swollen to the size of a grapefruit.

The Major saw it immediately and swore. "For God's sake!"

He looked around for someone human or equine to blame, but by then, everyone was moving off and there was no blame to be laid.

"Well, Bonfire, we will ride to our billet anyway, and that will keep it from getting stiff at least. Sorry, old chap."

He rubbed my ears by way of apology. Ear rubs made up for almost any transgression. I resolved to just buck up and get on with it. Within a mile or two it did feel better, just to be moving in any case. We hadn't ridden out since days ago in Devizes. I was soon enjoying it so much that I forgot the injury, for awhile at least.

EIGHT

The countryside was flat as a billiard table but lush. We were in the middle of farmland: dairy and beef cattle, sheep and vegetables. At times, when the wind was just right, a powerful smell of manure for fertilizing the spring crops wafted to us. It didn't smell like our horse or cow manure at home either but had an extra sharp tang to it that I couldn't identify. Not chicken. Not pig. I was familiar with those. Hmmm.

In time, this mystery substance would be known, and was part of a toxic cocktail that affected men who were wounded in the field. But that would be in days and weeks to come.

What we did begin to see plainly, the further we travelled north, was the damage from the fighting in the fall of 1914, and recent battles too. Many buildings had been damaged or ruined completely and reduced to nothing but piles of rubble. The locals appeared dour as they matter-of-factly went about their tasks. Their lives had been turned upside down, but you wouldn't know it from their demeanour.

At one stop The Major dressed my wound, which was still infected and quite sore. Lieutenant Helmer was riding with us and stood by watching. The Major then came toward me with a huge hypodermic syringe. I dreaded the sight of it, shut my eyes tightly and hung my head just wanting it to be over. I heard Lex chuckle.

"Look, Major," said Lex. "Look how he's hanging his head. He looks like a school boy about to get a licking." The Major laughed.

"There there, Bonfire," he said to me. "Do you think I would ever do anything to hurt The Chestnut Gentleman? Of course not."

The needle wasn't bad at all. He patted my rump several times, quite hard first, which sort of numbed it, and then gave me the shot.

"You see? Nothing to it, and that should help it heal."

Dodge, standing nearby with raised eyebrows, held up his bottle of castor oil elixir.

"Oh, right," said The Major, "I forgot about that stuff. Well, the shot should do the trick but Dodge, put some oil on it too. Let's hedge our bets."

We rode on and a new and pungent smell, sickly sweet, went up my nostrils, unnerving me. It made me feel panicky, like maybe I should bolt. We came around a bend, and saw the source of it up ahead, alongside the road. The odour emanated from two dead and bloated work horses, their harnesses still on and their wagon on its side, smashed to so much kindling. The horses lay on their sides, their top legs sticking stiffly out. The Major had to do some persuasive riding to make me go past. I just did not want to smell it anymore, and I certainly didn't want to look at it either. The Colonel's horse was of the same mind, so Colonel Morrison had his work cut out too. I'm sorry to say that we horses became well accustomed to such smells and sights within days. And in the weeks to come, we became used to even worse things.

* * *

As we travelled, the road north became more and more congested with horses, wagons, trucks, equipment and soldiers on the march, both mounted and on foot in great numbers. The entire CEF was making its way north toward the front. While we rested at one point, an infantry lieutenant of the 10th Battalion approached The Major with two injured privates in his charge. The soldiers of the 10th were from the Calgary and Winnipeg areas.

"Excuse me, Major, I'm told you're a doctor. Is this true?"

"Yes, Lieutenant. What can I do for you? Looks like these men need treatment." The Major came to me and untied his medical kit from my saddle.

The two men, a stocky, red-haired fellow and a tall, striking Native man, both had bloody arms with small bits of debris sticking out of their flesh. To me, they looked embarrassed rather than hurt. The Native man had a wood and sinew lacrosse racket in his hand and nervously spun it around and around on its end in the dirt.

The red-haired man started to speak, but The Major held up his hand.

"Don't tell me...prematurely exploding jam-jar grenades. Am I right?"

The two men were surprised and grinned sheepishly. Both of them nodded.

"Well, never mind. If that's the quality of weapons we've been reduced to, such things will happen."

The Major opened his small kit and took out tweezers and disinfectant.

He examined each man in turn and said, "Hmm, looks a bloody mess, but there's nothing bad enough for stitching. I'll just pick all these bits out, and you fellows," he said sternly, looking up at them, "keep these wounds clean! Do you hear me?"

"Yes, Major," the men said in unison.

Just then I noticed The Colonel–he was observing the whole thing with a little grin on his face. He whispered to Cosgrave, who was sitting on the grass beside him. "Brings me right back to some of his field doctoring from South African days."

As The Major picked out bits of metal, he wiped each cut and scrape with disinfectant. He asked the men, "What are your names and where are you from?"

"Private Red Hay from Elnora, Alberta, sir."

"Private Lionel Crowshoe from Stand-Off, Alberta, Major."

The Major finished up by winding clean gauze around the men's arms and taping it securely. He put the gauze, tweezers and scissors back into the little leather kit.

"Well, Hay and Crowshoe, that's that." He nodded at Crowshoe's lacrosse racket. "Do you play? My father was a dab hand at it. Won medals and everything. I thought the game hadn't made its way out west."

Private Crowshoe said simply, "Father Jean Lafontaine of Trois-Riviéres, Quebec, sir."

The Major nodded knowingly, "Ah hah. That explains it. Well, you men take care of yourselves, and I hope never to see you again," he said with pretend sternness, but there was a twinkle in his eye.

The privates smiled broadly as he shook their hands in turn, and I couldn't help noticing what a kind way he had with them. The young men began to walk back down the road to where their huge battalion,

The Fighting 10th, was starting to form up again for the march toward the front.

"And, boys," The Major called out after them. They stopped and turned around. "You might want to rethink your launching device." He nodded toward the lacrosse racket in Private Crowshoe's hand.

Both men grinned, and Crowshoe made an extravagant overhand stroke with the racket. Then they turned and walked on. They seemed like nice boys, and I hoped those would be their only injuries.

Soon The Colonel stood up and mounted King. He gave the order for us to move out, and we were on the march again. Next stop, and what would become our HQ for several days, the village of Meteren, France.

* * *

The Major, The Colonel and Cosgrave and we three horses moved into our billet, a lovely little house in Meteren inhabited by an elderly woman, Madame d'Ailly, and her middle-aged daughter, Monique. This was when I made another discovery about The Major. I was in the stable in back of the house, and Monique was spoiling me with a special type of very hard and crunchy ginger cookie that I just could not get enough of.

The Major appeared and said, "Bonjour, Monique. Comment ça va?"

And off they went into a long spiel in the French language. I had no idea. Even though I grew up in Quebec, it seemed that the fox-hunting crowd was only anglophone, or English speaking, and I seldom heard the French language. The Major always surprised me with what he knew.

The little house in Meteren was a welcome change from all the places we had stayed in since Valcartier. The two women were friendly, comical and just great company. I found this surprising in light of what had been happening all around them with the war. Madame d'Ailly gave out nicknames to both The Major and Captain Cosgrave. She called The Major, La Médecine Major (The Medicine Major) and Cosgrave, Le Bébé (The Baby), because he was only twenty-five but already a captain. The Colonel had always called the young captain "Cosgrave," or sometimes "Moore," his middle name; Lawrence Moore Cosgrave. But he always referred to him as The Baby after that. The nickname stayed with him for the duration of the war.

From our billet in Meteren, not too far south of the Belgian border, The Major and I and Colonel Morrison and King rode out daily to check out the area, check on our batteries and gun lines and try to get as good of a look at the war as possible, without getting shot at or shelled. We had four batteries with four guns each. Things were relatively quiet at this point. Sporadic, distant shelling and gunfire was continuous. No actual battle was taking place yet, but tension was building toward a big offensive, and it would be our first battle, although we would not be in the thick of it. We would be on the flank supporting the British, who had already been fighting for almost seven months at this point.

One day The Major was asked to go a few miles away to see to a soldier who had been kicked in the stomach. We rode out on our own on a beautiful spring morning. It was sad to see all the fresh graves of soldiers everywhere, sometimes in the most haphazard places, as though they'd been buried right where they had fallen.

The Major noticed one grave in particular on the edge of a tiny and ancient village cemetery. He remarked what a mess it was, and why didn't someone at least tidy up the weeds? The grave was a mound of black earth with a tangle of what looked like dead plants or flowers over the top of it. At the back of it was a white wooden cross with hand-drawn words on it: Pvt. Harold Garner, Durham Light Infantry, Died Dec.16, 1914. That was only a a couple of months earlier.

We rode on and soon could hear a motorcar approaching. Then we could see the vehicle, and there were two soldiers in it: a driver and passenger in the back seat. As it got closer, I felt The Major tense up, and he spoke.

"Damn it, Bonfire," he said, patting my neck a couple of times. "It's that infernal Carleton Jones." I still wasn't sure what the source of their acrimony was.

The large, open motor car pulled up, and General Jones got out and walked up to us. Without any sort of greeting or any preamble at all, which I thought exceedingly rude, he went on the attack.

"McCrae, what is this nonsense about the war hospital here being run by McGill and even being called a 'McGill' hospital?! Who the hell does your Birkett think he is?"

Herbert Birkett was a close colleague of the Major's, a dear friend, and the dean of medicine at McGill University Medical School in Montreal. He was in the process of setting up what would become a crucial hospital for treating thousands of soldiers–not just Canadians, but soldiers of all the countries involved.

"How jolly to see you, Jones," said The Major with a tone of sarcasm I hadn't heard from him before. "What brings you out on this grand, sunny morning?"

Jones stared at The Major in silence for a disturbingly long few seconds.

"Major McCrae, if I wanted to remove you from here, I could, and I could install you anywhere I like if it suits–"

The Major cut him off.

"General Jones, you need to know that I do not give a snap about army medical corps promotions or matters as I am not a part of that

73

unholy band of . . . of that organization. I have been gazetted to the artillery, and Colonel Morrison got permission to appoint me to this position from Minister Hughes. If you continue to have a problem with it, I suggest you take up the matter with the Minister."

General Jones stood and seethed for a few more seconds. Then he spoke quietly, venomously.

"As you know, McCrae, medicals are not allowed to have horses. I've said it before; don't get too fond of that animal."

With that, General Jones spun around and strode to the motorcar. His last words sent a chill down the length of my spine. The Major was as tense as steel and said under his breath, "I am not a bloody medical officer and he needs to get that through his thick skull." I could feel his anger, but there was a touch of fear there too. Maybe he got the same chill as me.

Before the General could even get settled into the car, The Major urged me into a canter away down the road, and we kicked up clods of muck in their general direction as we left. After a good run, he calmed down and we came to the farm where the man who had been kicked was billeted.

The Major sat at the bedside and asked the man, a private from Nova Scotia, "Where were you kicked, son?"

The soldier was weak and very white. He put his hand on his stomach. His sergeant whispered, "He went to the toilet, sir, and there was a lot of blood."

The Major stood up and said, "That's a blighty," which was a nickname for a wound that could get you out of the war. Blighty was also what soldiers called England sometimes. "You need to get him on a hospital train for England at once. Can you do that, Sergeant? He may be fit in a few weeks, but right now, and I mean as soon as

Snowdrops in France

possible," The Major said with force, "he will need surgery before he becomes septic. Are we clear?"

"Yes, sir," said the sergeant.

The Major patted the sick man on the shoulder. "You'll be alright, son. You'll be taken care of right away."

The Major prepared to mount up as the sergeant came running to our side.

"Sir, will he be alright? Really?"

The Major sighed. "Only if you can get him onto an operating table within twenty-four hours. Can you do that?"

"I think so, Major. I'll do my best."

The Major softened. "That's all any of us can do. Even if I had the tools . . . but I don't. Go to it, Sergeant. There's no time to waste."

We rode back by the little graveyard we'd passed in the morning. The fresh grave with the tangle of weeds had been transformed. We were both touched to see that delicate white snowdrops had burst into bloom on top of the soldier's grave, and the tangle of weeds was actually a cluster of snowdrops that some kind friend had planted in the shape of a cross.

* * *

At the beginning of March we left our lovely billet in Meteren. The Major, The Colonel and Cosgrave shook hands with our hosts, and I was very sad to say goodbye to Madame d'Ailly and Monique (and her ginger cookies). The entire brigade moved back a little south again, into the area around Fleurbaix, where we were to be posted for an entire month. Our brigade took over for a British brigade, and we were to support them on their flank. A big surprise attack was slated for March 10, 1915.

I was coming to realize just how fortunate I was to be with an officer. King and I were put into a tidy stable behind the Major's new billet. It was another quaint cottage, a farmhouse, where The Major, The Colonel and Cosgrave had comfortable rooms and beds again. My leg was almost completely healed, and I was feeling happy and frisky. The weather was beautiful, flowers were blooming and it was almost possible to forget there was a war on. Until artillery fire boomed again.

The other horses and mules were tied in lines like in Valcartier and Salisbury Plain, but at least they were not being assaulted by wind and rain. Staying outside was just fine for now.

Although we Canadians were not in the thick of the fighting, the soldiers still had to be vigilant. Many of the wounds that did occur were wounds to the head. German snipers were beginning to take a toll.

The Major and The Colonel went to a village church tower to try to get a bird's-eye view of the area and had to quickly get down and stay down while a sniper tried to pick them off.

A particularly troublesome sharpshooter killed an infantry soldier of the 10th Battalion and injured several of our men. With binoculars, The Major discovered that the sniper was shooting from the second floor of a damaged and abandoned farmhouse. The Major and Captain Cosgrave directed one of our guns to fire on the house and scored a direct hit, completely caving in what was left of the second floor. That sniper was stopped, but there were always more to take his place.

The British brass chastised Colonel Morrison for using too many shells. A messenger arrived and ordered The Colonel to a nearby palatial chateau being used as their HQ. Later, The Colonel told The Major that he had stood in front of a large desk behind which sat three English generals.

He told us, putting on a posh English accent, "One of them actually said, 'Colonel, we cannot have you firing off shells willy-nilly, whenever the mood takes you.'"

He was funny, and angry at the same time. I knew he was angry because he asked Captain Cosgrave for a cigarette. He rarely smoked, and never carried them himself.

He continued. "I told him that there was a whole Boche (a nickname for the Germans) battery, strolling la-de-da across an open field toward us with four guns, and what did he expect me to do? Invite them for tea? I ordered Major Britten to deal with them."

We Canadians were then rationed to three shells per gun per day.

The Colonel was incensed, and he ranted to The Major, "They are treating us like children. What in the bloody hell are we here for if we can't shoot our guns?!"

Days later, we found out the rationing was partly due to a shortage of fuses.

Another infantry soldier was brought to The Major for treatment after he had been shot in the ear. Luckily it was "a graze" alongside his head, but what The Major learned about the cause of it was unsettling. The man, a skinny private from Princeton, British Columbia, told him what happened as The Major dabbed at his bloody ear with a cloth soaked in disinfectant.

"I was firing my Ross from the fire-step in our trench and the bayonet fell off. It just popped off, right over the parapet. Then I tried to pop over into No Man's Land and grab it, and that's when they shot me."

The Major kept on working.

Then the man said, "Major, it happens all the time with the Ross rifle. I'm not the only one."

I, myself, did not like gunfire anywhere near my head although I could just about tolerate it. But the big guns, the eighteen pounders and howitzers of the 1st Brigade and all the big field guns were always nerve-jangling, and it was beyond an assault on the ears. It rattled our very bones and shook us right down into our hearts.

Another and even worse failing of the Ross rifle had also recently become apparent. When any of the men were rapid-firing it, their bullets would jam in the gun as soon as it began to heat. They would then have to bash on the bolt to move it, either with their boot or shovel. This was alarming news. At the moment, the men were in trenches and only supporting the British on the edge of the fight in a minor way. But The Major immediately saw how this jamming could be catastrophic once our men were in a major battle of their own, especially if they were ever in the open without good cover.

Some of the men grabbed a solid and efficient, British-made, Lee-Enfield rifle when they could and would leave a Ross in its place. But the officers soon discovered this and forbade it under threat of severe punishment. The Canadians would be stuck with the Ross rifle for awhile yet.

An objective overview made me realize that so far, our men were flying by the seats of their pants in this war. They were fighting without helmets and just had little wool wedge caps on their heads. They were fighting with unpredictable, homemade jam-jar grenades, bayonets that fell off of rifles that routinely jammed, a shortage of artillery shells due to a shortage of fuses and last but not least, an entrenching tool with a hole in it. I decided to only think about problems as they came up, and if The Major didn't seem to mind, then neither would I. I resolved not to take an objective overview again.

* * *

Sir Sam Hughes with the MacAdams shovel

March 10 began with an incredible, utterly deafening artillery barrage by the British at Neuve-Chapelle. Our brigade was still at Fleurbaix, which was five miles up the road, and from there we continued to support the British flank by firing on sniper houses, on the German trenches and occasionally on the enemy, when they tried to move about in the open.

The Major was kept especially busy with medical duties once the battle started. He would be called to the gun lines by telephone if there was a casualty.

Cosgrave came by and The Major told him, "I found an arm this morning on the road. Just an arm, a uniformed arm in a pool of blood."

Most of the injuries to men in the trenches were to the head. These injuries were caused either by sniper fire or shrapnel shells that burst above the trenches and showered their contents onto the men from above.

The Battle of Neuve-Chapelle ended with our men acquitting themselves well, given their limitations. One hundred Canadian soldiers were killed. It was a different story for the British. They suffered thirteen thousand casualties, and the battle ended in a stalemate.

After a day of patching up wounded men, The Major walked toward me. His appearance was usually neat and tidy, but today he was bleary eyed and stubble faced. He dropped his medical bag on the ground and put his arms around me, burying his face deep in my neck, and just stood there like that for several seconds. I could hear his breathing again. It crackled and squeaked with each breath in.

* * *

We got our orders to march north. After a month in Fleurbaix, France, we were on the move again, and this time our destination was northwestern Belgium, and the fields of Flanders.

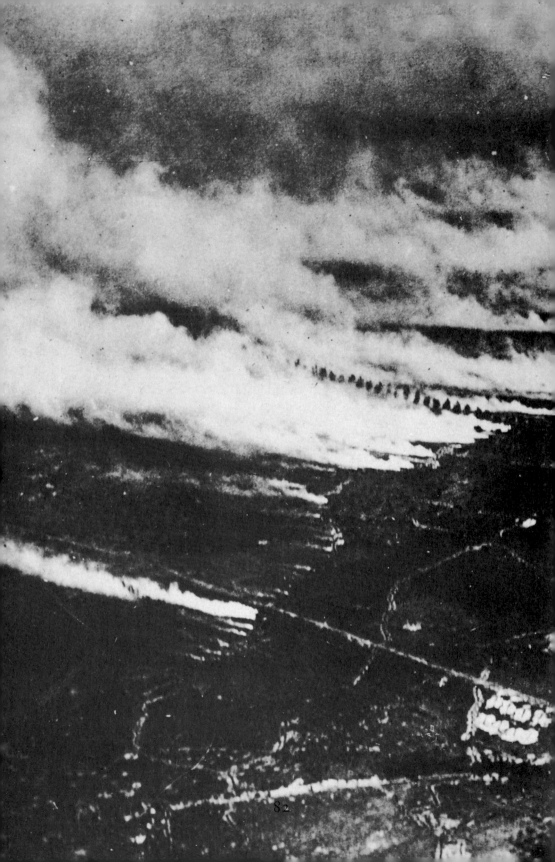

PART FOUR
COMETH THE NIGHT

NINE

After a month in the trenches and various billets, it took a bit of organizing to form up into a complete column. Once that was achieved, we began the march north for Belgium. We were an impressive sight; almost nine hundred men, most marching on foot, and over six hundred horses carrying officers and pulling limbers, guns and supply wagons. And let us not forget the mules. The Major and I were in the front with The Colonel and King, and our brigade stretched back down the road behind us as far as we could see.

It was a glorious spring day, sunny and mild, and after a good night's sleep and a wash and shave, The Major was back to his cheery self again. In full voice, and a deep bass tone like his laugh, he began his song:

"The Minstrel boy to the war has gone, / In the ranks of death you'll find him, / His father's sword he hath girded on / And his wild harp slung behind him. / Land of song! sung the warrior bard, / Tho' all the world betray thee. / One sword at least thy rights shall guard, / One faithful heart shall praise thee . . . "

At this point, he was completely drowned out by almost all the men when they broke into "The Maple Leaf Forever."

The Colonel raised his eyebrows at this and then he, Cosgrave and Lex laughed at The Major's feigned indignation at being upstaged.

It was quite a jolly group, and there wasn't too much evidence of war just then, just last fall's damage and the very occasional and distant sound of artillery from the northeast.

Once the men had finished the song and it was quiet again, The Colonel said, "McCrae, sing us that one from the Karoo. You know, that mushy one you used to do round the fire at night."

The Major thought for a minute and then said, "Oh, I know the one." He cleared his throat and began:

"Drink to me only with thine eyes, / And I will pledge with mine. / Or leave a kiss within the cup / And I will not ask for wine."

This time both Cosgrave and Lex raised their eyebrows and looked at each other, as they'd never seen this side of The Major. The Colonel, on the other hand, closed his eyes and tipped his head from side to side in time as he listened. The Major continued.

"The thirst that from the soul doth rise, / Doth ask a drink divine. / But might I of Jove's nectar sip . . . "

86

And then he was drowned out completely when the men launched into "O Canada." They all broke up laughing, including The Major. Then he made a face and shouted loudly, "Oh, what's the use!" which made the other men laugh harder.

And on we went.

* * *

On April 19 we arrived in Poperinghe, Belgium, deep in the west of Flanders. We billeted in and around the beer-making town, which for the time had become a busy hub for soldiers and equipment going into and out of the war. There began to be whisperings about a battle taking shape, an offensive that we would launch from this town.

On April 20 some of our brigade went forward and reconnoitered positions northeast of the beautiful, medieval, cloth-trading city of Ypres. These were positions that were currently being held by French batteries. It was known that the German Army expected to take this city, sweep down and then capture Paris. It was our job to stop them.

It seemed that the excitement of the men was giving way to a kind of grim resolve, with a healthy undercurrent of fear. Or maybe that was just me. I looked at our fresh-faced young soldiers–students, clerks, farmers, salesmen. What did they know about war? They'd had a little taste in Fleurbaix, but here they were, on the eve of a real battle that they would be in the middle of this time.

As for me, I had the creeping feeling that Bonfire, Fox Hunter Extraordinaire, was about to earn his keep as a proper war horse, whether he liked it or not. It was time to let go of the fox hunter moniker forever. It seemed so frivolous now.

The men did some drilling and marching. The officers wanted to keep them fit and sharp, but that wasn't easy. They wanted to let off steam after their long month in the trenches around Fleurbaix. Keeping them out of Poperinghe's many cafés and bars, with their strong, locally brewed beer and pretty girls was a full-time job.

Well, we all had to smarten up when Poperinghe was hit with several bombs on the morning of April 22. There was some building damage and not much else, but it was as though the Germans were sending us an explosive message, a taste of what was to come.

TEN

On April 22, the Germans began a terrific bombardment of Ypres. What had happened to Poperinghe that morning was nothing compared to the assault on the beautiful city. By the afternoon, we had been ordered to march toward Ypres but were made to halt alongside the road a few miles away and await orders. Every six minutes, a one-ton shell was fired into the centre of Ypres. The destruction was beyond imagining. The great Cloth Hall that had stood in the centre of the city since the thirteenth century was being dismantled, hundreds of bricks at a time, as each shell scored a direct hit. The heart of Ypres was being torn out.

This is to say nothing of the civilian casualties as the shells rained down. This non-military target that had the audacity to stand up to the great German Army and refuse it passage was now paying the price in human terms that were indescribable. As we assembled on the side of the road and waited for our orders, The Major became angrier by the minute. The magnificent Cloth Hall could be seen across the flat fields to our right, and it was disappearing before our eyes. What remained standing was on fire with towering flames that leapt into the night sky.

On the road before us, hordes of civilians ran for their lives: whole and fractured families, mothers with babies, small crying children, the elderly, and injured and bandaged people. Some travelled with horse- or dog-drawn wagons with all their worldly possessions heaped on top. They had gathered whatever they could quickly grab and take before, and sometimes after, the bombs hit their houses. A teenaged boy pushed his ancient, crippled grandfather in a rickety wheelbarrow. Another skinny teen jockey-backed his grandmother, his spindly legs nearly collapsing under the weight. A young woman with ghostly, vacant eyes protectively carried a baby that I believe was already dead, its head hanging backward at an unnatural angle.

Some were crying, others stoic as they escaped the onslaught. It was chaos. As we waited, the 10th Battalion appeared beside us, weaving its way through the masses moving toward it, in its effort to march to the front. We spied Hay and Crowshoe on the far side of a crush of fleeing civilians. They recognized us, smiled and smartly saluted as they marched eastward, heading for the front. Hay was easy to spot with his thatch of bright red hair sticking out from under his wedge cap. Crowshoe still had the lacrosse racket, now tied onto the back of his rucksack.

As the afternoon wore on, a tremendous artillery barrage commenced to the distant northeast, and still the bombs sailed into Ypres too. And we sat, waited and waited. Waited for our orders. The Major would leave me with Dodge every so often and offer medical treatment where he could–bandage a wound, or create a makeshift sling.

All the men were getting impatient, including The Major. It was as if all the men wanted to go, now, and try to stop the atrocity unfolding before us.

A snappy-looking British infantry regiment came along the road behind us, from the west. They marched along and sang, "It's a long way to Tipperary, / It's a long way to go . . ." and off they went eastward and right into the thick of it. What would become of them? What would become of us all?

Unexpectedly, soldiers began to appear from the north on our left. Some were French soldiers with bright red pants and blue tunics. But most were North African, French colonial soldiers in puffy trousers with strange hats on; Turcos, Zouaves, Moroccans. Across the flat fields they ran; some on foot, some on horses and some heaped on wagons. A black draught horse came toward us with his harness still on and three men on his broad back. Some of the men were in hysterics.

A junior French officer, missing his hat and his horse, ran by us shouting as he passed, "All is lost! Everything is lost!" He ran on westward down the road.

Then the smell hit us. The Major and The Colonel looked at each other in alarm. The Major said one word: "Chlorine!"

"By God, I did not believe they would use it," said Colonel Morrison angrily. "I refused to believe the rumours."

Lex Helmer came riding up with eyes like saucers. "Major, is it gas? Chlorine gas?!"

"It is, son," said The Major. He shook his head and stared at the dishevelled French soldiers. "Good Lord, did you ever see such a debacle?"

Just then an Algerian Zouave fell off the back of a wagon heaped with fleeing French soldiers and landed on the cobblestones with a slap. The driver snapped the reins, urged the horses on and did not stop or even look back. The man began to convulse on the side of the road. The Major jumped off me, and Dodge took my reins while The Major grabbed his kit. He ran to the man and then just stood over him helplessly as the man thrashed about wildly and tore at his throat. Then yellowish foam came out of the man's mouth and nose, and he quickly turned blue. Then he was still.

The Major turned and looked at us. I don't know how to describe the look he had on his face; it was similar to the helpless rage he had displayed on Salisbury Plain, when we were turned out of the wood in the storm, only worse. Then he put his arms under the man's arms and dragged him off into the ditch. He walked back to us wheezing and coughing. He had been mildly gassed himself, just by standing over the dying man, and he smelled strongly of it.

"At least I can spare him the indignity of being run over."

He mounted again and sat in silence. No one knew what to say about any of it. Who had ever fought gas clouds? Who would use such a . . . a . . . low weapon. Certainly not our army. But that would change too, in the coming weeks, and be justified as fighting fire with fire.

The mobs of fleeing French soldiers began running against us with the westward-moving civilians, causing further chaos. Another big draught horse on his own, sweat-soaked with harness on, came staggering across the field on our left. His sides were heaving and that same yellowish foam was oozing out of his nostrils. The big horse got onto the road and stumbled dangerously through the civilians until Lex jumped off his horse and grabbed his bridle. He led him off the road, lifted his forelock and shot him in the forehead with his sidearm. His legs buckled under him, and the massive animal collapsed heavily. Lex returned to his own horse and mounted as he blinked back tears. We all knew it was the only thing to do for the poor beast. The Major nodded at him in a gesture of compassion and respect for the young man. He'd done an extremely difficult but timely and necessary thing.

The Colonel became increasingly agitated. He turned to The Major. "I'm going to go forward to try to see what the hell is going on. Even if we get orders to move, how will we move with this?!" He motioned to the mob in front of us. "Bloody hell. We need to go to it, and we need to go, now," said The Colonel.

He urged King forward and people just had to get out of his way. The road was dead straight, the terrain flat and we could still see him a mile up due to the glow of shell fire and the burning Cloth Hall. Also, the Germans regularly sent up "star shells," which lit up the sky like day.

Then a British officer rode up to Colonel Morrison, and the two men briefly conferred. They both turned and rode back to us. It was Major Beatty of the British Royal Artillery. The time to move out was now, and not a moment to waste.

We were told to take a position behind the dyke, along the Yser Canal about two miles straight north of Ypres. It was 3:45 a.m., and we were to be there and start digging in within half an hour. We would be part of a massive counterattack against the enemy's bombardment of Ypres, and the gas.

* * *

Captain Cosgrave, Lieutenant Helmer and a few other soldiers created a wedge into the throng of civilians and pitiful French soldiers running toward us. We needed our own channel through the traffic so we could get to our position. Soon the crowds thinned and The Major urged me into a gallop. There was no time to lose. Our mission was to stop the giant German Army from marching through Ypres, and we were sworn to do it.

The ride itself was hair-raising enough, and we hadn't even gotten into position yet. We had to dodge people, carts and wagons, and all the while deafening shells rained into Ypres on our right and a small village now to our left. We reached the Yser Canal, which ran north to south, took a sharp left turn and headed north again. It was still two miles to our spot.

Bunkers in the back of the dyke beside the Yser Canal near Essex Farm

A quarter mile short of the position behind the dyke along the canal, The Major left me with Dodge at a farm and put me in a pen there. King was already there as The Colonel had gone ahead by a few minutes, to scout the position. The Major ran off as fast as his legs would carry him. The human occupants of the farm had fled but there were a few cows and chickens about. The cows were upset by it all, moaning and milling about in a small, adjoining pasture. This would not last long. A shell exploded close to them and they panicked, crashed through their fence and scattered into the night.

I felt helpless and quite terrified in our pen and backed into the furthest corner from where the shells seemed to originate. King, on the other hand, was agitated and paced back and forth, back and forth, along the eastern fence. He strained his head and neck as he tried to see what was going on along the canal, but it was too dark just then. It helped some to have Dodge with us, but he was a worried mess as well. At least our food and water needs were attended to.

ELEVEN

hat follows is based upon my own experience and what I was able to glean afterwards. The Major would later refer to this period as *Seventeen days of Hades!*

There was not just one gas attack. The gas came down every couple of days, and when it wasn't the awful greenish-yellow chlorine cloud drifting across us, it was gas shells exploding around us, a sort of tear gas I believe. Every time I smelled any of it, it would sicken me, and I'd experience a sharp twinge of worry for The Major with his asthma. The gas made Dodge vomit so often that I was fearful for his health too.

We were not too far at all from the canal, and in daylight, we could see a lot of what was happening. During the day, enemy aeroplanes flew over regularly and spied on the brigade. I was sure they were gathering information that could only hurt us.

Our brigade had four batteries of four field guns each. The first night we went in, numbers 1 and 4 were back in reserve, which was not a good thing. They were all desperately needed. Soon they were all brought up and firing continuously. They had to be constantly moved because the enemy would pin-point their positions and fire on them quite precisely. This was the beginning of terrible losses of our men in the firing lines. I'm pretty sure the aeroplanes helped with that. In my lifetime, I had never imagined that I would see little machines that could fly about in the air overhead.

The noise. There are just no words at all to describe the constant din of artillery cannons, theirs and ours. It made every nerve jangle, even Dodge's. There was no getting used to it. There are also no words at all to describe what an artillery shell does to a living thing. Imagine something, say, the size of a milk bottle, but jagged, irregular shaped. A white-hot piece of metal slamming into a living body. Whole pieces were taken off; legs, arms, heads. Then there were shrapnel shells, filled with hundreds of marble-sized lead balls that were designed to explode above trenches and shower their deadly payload onto the men below. Diabolical creations of war.

Farmhouses across the canal to the east, where the enemy were firing from, were all destroyed and burned to the ground along with their beautiful windmills. Most of the farmhouses on our side were, too. Ours had been hit but was still standing, so we stayed where we were.

The Major had an eight-by-eight-foot hole dug into the dirt of the steep, west side of the dyke along the canal. He got it shored up with scraps of metal and timber and it overlooked the main road that ran north out of Ypres. This was where he spent most of the seventeen days of the battle, where he did his utmost to attend to the overwhelming hordes of wounded: our men, French colonial troops from North Africa and the British.

The Major was under orders to treat only men brought to him, but he defied Colonel Morrison's orders. At great peril to himself, he repeatedly went onto the road and dragged injured men off to safety, and he saved the lives of several wounded horses as well. I felt I could almost see him across the fields, but it was hard to be sure. In time, there were several dugouts in a row there, along the back of the dyke.

One morning I was sure I did see him in the distance. There was heavy shelling going on, and he ran, carrying his medical kit, across an open field to the west, toward our rear gun lines. Someone at the guns must have been injured. A couple of times he flung himself down in the dirt when shells landed close. It was worrying to watch. You could hear the shells coming, too. Each type of shell had a signature whine or whistle. And above all this racket, the little larks flew high above or sat in the hedges and remaining poplars and sang as sweetly as ever.

The Colonel, on the other hand, was on the move continually. He spent much of the battle forward on the east side of the canal, across the pontoon bridge and on the most dangerous grounds of all, where the troops were in their trenches. There he did his best to support the infantry by selecting enemy targets and having them destroyed with our field guns. The Canadians had strung themselves out thinly where the French had been routed by the gas, but there was a continuous fear that that line would break too, under such ferocious pressure from the enemy.

Times of quiet were extremely rare, but when it was silent, we slept heavily. Dodge stayed in the open with King and me. He made a sort of nest in the corner of our pen with straw, hay and his heavy, grey wool greatcoat for cover and warmth. It was as though he didn't want to let us out of his sight.

The battle raged on and on. Horse- and mule-drawn supply wagons kept our men in ammunition and occasionally food. But they were often unlucky. The enemy artillery sometimes shelled them, and there was nothing worse for King and me than hearing one of our own scream. The Major was of the same mind. Later he would say, "There was nothing I hated hearing more than that horse scream."

Even when the artillery was quieter at night, streams of gunfire swept the dyke, and the men had to be vigilant at all times.

* * *

NORTH

1st Brigade CFA position
2 miles north of Ypres

GAS

CEMETERY

APRIL 22 - MAY 8, 1945
The 2nd Battle of Ypres

Yser Canal

WEST

EAST

ESSEX FARM

SOUTH

Aerial photograph of Essex Farm taken approximately 27 April, 1915

The Canadians were involved in scores of heroic and desperate actions that we would hear about later. The 10th Battalion and the 16th Canadian Scottish were in a tremendous battle for Kitcheners Wood. I thought of Privates Hay and Crowshoe in the 10th from Alberta often and wondered about their welfare. We heard the 10th lost over three quarters of its men.

* * *

May 2 was the most terrible day. A focussed and terrific enemy barrage began first thing in the morning and rained shells on our brigade. Back in our pen, King and I tried to eat our respective little piles of hay that Dodge had set out for us, just a few feet apart, but it was all but impossible to relax enough to eat.

Suddenly, there was a tremendous explosion, so close that I instantly found I could not hear. The pen filled with smoke, so I couldn't see either, and I admit that panic overtook me. Then a strong, sudden wind gust cleared the smoke, and where King had stood beside me eating, there were only some jagged scraps of dapple-grey hide, a hoof and some bones strewn about that I couldn't make sense of. King was no more. How could this be?! He'd been standing right beside me. My mind raced crazily as I tried to make sense of it.

Dodge ran toward me, but I bolted and leapt straight over the fence and out of the pen. I was out of my mind with fear, and I ran hard and fast with no thought for the direction I was going. I thought my heart would hammer right out of my chest. Suddenly I saw the dyke. Maybe I could find The Major . . . but wait. There was a familiar form. It was Lex! He stood on the side of the road, talking to another young officer. He saw me, and his eyes widened with shock. He knew I was not supposed to be anywhere near the fighting or firing lines. He began to turn toward me, and it seemed as though time slowed and stretched out just as there was another tremendous BOOM. The young officer Lex had been talking to fell, severely hit in the thighs.

And young lieutenant Alexis Hannum Helmer vanished before my eyes in a blood-tinted cloud of smoke and human debris. He had met the same fate as King and had been blown into oblivion. Instantly I wheeled and thundered back the way I had come. I took to the Brielen Road westward and almost immediately came upon a mangled team of four horses and their wagon, down and strewn across the road. There was nowhere to go but over them. After skittering on the pavement over the wagon's spilled load of eighteen-pound shells, I gathered myself, leapt over the wagon and galloped on.

I was well down the road and still running when it hit me. The lead horse I had seen down on the driver's side was a sleek, dark bay with a distinctive sliver of a crescent moon on his forehead. It was Thor.

I did not stop for miles, not until I feared my heart would burst if I ran another step.

* * *

This is what I heard happened after Lex's death. The Major ordered the soldiers to pick up every bit of Lex Helmer they could. The soldiers put all the remains they could find into a couple of burlap sacks. Then, those sacks were placed onto a single army blanket. Once they'd pinned it all together into a semblance of a human shape, they buried what was left of young Lex Helmer in the little cemetery beside the canal. No chaplains were about so The Major said the service over him as well as he could from memory. It was said a tiny picture had been found nearby of Lex's fiancée in Canada with a hole through it, right where her heart would have been. They buried it with Lex.

Sometime over the next couple of days, blood-red poppies began to spring out of the churned-up soil everywhere. The Major was taking a brief break from his duties when he noticed that poppies had burst out of the ground all around Lex's grave, their red heads gently bobbing in the spring breeze. Words for a poem came to him spontaneously, and he grabbed his notebook and started to write:

The ruined Cloth Hall of Ypres in 1916

"In Flanders Fields the poppies blow. / Between the crosses, row on row, / That mark our place . . . "

The young fellow Lex had been talking to when he was hit, Lieutenant Owen Hague, had been rushed out by field ambulance, but he died later of his wounds.

* * *

As for me, Dodge came and found me almost two days later. I had, sensibly, stayed on a westward path of travel, away from the canal and the fighting and had taken refuge at another abandoned farm several miles away. When Dodge found me I was actually sleeping, the sleep of the dead, I might add, in a stall with its door wide open.

"Oh, Master Bonfire. Thank God, you're alright," Dodge exclaimed. "I don't think The Major could have stood the loss of Lex and you, too. Oh, thank God, thank God."

Dodge led me to another farm in between the first one we'd been at and this one. Every so often he would look at me and pat me on the neck as we walked and just quietly whisper, "Thank God."

As we walked I ruminated. There would be no thanking God for Lex Helmer, or King either, for that matter. How was it possible that King could have been obliterated, only mere feet from me? And here walked I, still in good form. It was not fair, and it made no sense.

I learned that this was a terrible, terrible question, and one that would plague most of the soldiers and beasts who survived the Great War to the very end of their days. *Why him and not me?*

For myself, I decided that I would do my best to conduct my life with honour for all my days and be grateful for every day, and every friend, and every blade of grass, and every kernel of oats. Even though it made no sense to me. None of it. Not the reasons for the war or how it played out. I would not anguish over those things that I couldn't understand. I would forever hold the memory of those fallen men and beasts in my heart, and simply strive, always, to be worthy of them.

* * *

We prevented the Germans from coming into the city of Ypres at great cost to all of us. Still, their lines were getting closer and closer as they'd gained a lot of ground by using the gas. On May 9, 1915, we received orders to retire from our position and get out quickly with our men, horses, supplies and guns.

The men had to pull the guns out by hand. There was no time to bring up the horses. But when our last heavy supply wagon got hopelessly stuck in a ditch, The Colonel refused to let it go. He hollered, "Get those horses off and bring up the mules! Now!"

Gunner Jock Oliphant soon came running with Magnus and Monty harnessed together and hitched them to the wagon. "Haaah, Monty, Haaah," he shouted at the top of his lungs, and with Magnus's steadying, Monty's great strength came into play. Every muscle rippled as he strained forward, and within a couple of minutes, the wagon was dislodged and back rolling again.

God bless the mules. I would never speak disparagingly of them again. We got away almost completely without casualties. Just the very last wagon was hit and one horse was killed.

Dodge saddled me and then watched out for The Major because he no longer knew where we were. He left briefly and found him, and they walked together back to our new billet. My heart thumped with excitement at the thought of seeing my dear master again. Seventeen days had felt like seventeen weeks.

When they appeared, it was dusk, and they walked down the little country road toward me. I nickered a welcome. I couldn't quite see him, but when I finally did, I was rocked to my very soul. The Major had lost maybe ten or fifteen pounds. He was gaunt, pale, and now had an unkempt beard. *His uniform! Good grief.* It very nearly could stand by itself; stiff and soaked through with blood from top to bottom. His eyes were bloodshot, and when he laid eyes on me, they instantly brimmed with tears.

"Oh, Bonfire," was all he said as he walked up and flung his arms around my neck.

Dodge helped him mount, and he groaned as he settled stiffly into the saddle. We caught up with The Colonel, now on a new horse, and the rest of the brigade.

The Colonel looked sideways at The Major. "Well, Jack, I must say, we've looked better. We'll get some good rest now, for a few days anyway."

The Major nodded. "I suppose we saw the entire production, from the appetizers to the brandy and cigars." The Major paused and added, "I could use a brandy right about now"

The Colonel nodded, and we rode along in silence. I felt an unspoken pall cast over us all, with the death of Lex. But that wasn't all. The 1st Brigade Canadian Field Artillery had lost over two hundred men and more than a hundred horses, and this was only our first real battle.

TWELVE

We rode sixteen miles that night, and arrived at our billets in the early dawn. We had headed back south into France again, to Steenwerck, where we had first arrived off the train from St. Nazaire in February. What a relief to be with The Major again. In spite of the long ride, his mood and energy improved the further we got from the canal bank in Ypres. Still, it was shocking to see the state of the rest of the men and to realize that many of the familiar faces from earlier days had been invalided out on ambulance trains, or worse, were gone forever.

On our march south, we heard a terrible piece of news from a British cavalry major we met on the road. A ship called the Lusitania, full of holiday-makers, had just been sunk by a submarine off the coast of Ireland. Over a thousand were dead. This made both The Major and Colonel very angry. They didn't need any more bad news.

It wasn't until the second day south that The Major noticed the wound in my flank that had almost healed. It had been quite ugly and painful when I had first gotten it, but Dodge treated it and now it was mainly just a lumpy sort of scar. We were outside the barn at our billet, and Dodge was about to trim my hooves and give me new shoes.

"Private Dodge," The Major said, "just when were you going to tell me about Bonfire's little injury here?"

Dodge looked a little sheepish. "When that shell hit King, a small piece of metal must have hit Bonfire too. I didn't know it myself until I found him two days later. I bandaged him up at the time, and well, by the time we all got out of Ypres, it was pretty much healed. I didn't want to worry you with it, sir. Not after what you'd just come through. And anyway, it's almost as good as new. Isn't it, Master Bonfire?"

Dodge ran his hand over it as I picked his wedge cap off his head and flung it right over The Major's shoulder. Both men laughed, and that was a welcome sound, I can tell you.

"I can see he's back to himself. Maybe we should call him 'Gunfire,'" said The Major. The two men laughed again. Then he went silent. "Now I just have to get back to myself. Not sure when or if that will ever happen."

We settled into a restful few days in our billet. The men got showered and shaved, got new uniforms or parts of them, and new socks and underwear. Then they began to refit the guns which had been used and battered and beaten, almost into junk in some cases. We rode out around the batteries and then up to Plugstreet Wood, (proper Flemish spelling is Ploegsteert), where The Major and The Colonel had tea with some British Royal Artillery officers after they showed us the historic battle grounds there.

* * *

Our respite did not last. Before long, we had orders to move into battle near Festubert, France. I will only say that although short, it was a dirty battle in an ugly, dirty place. Unburied bodies were everywhere in various states of decomposition. *The all-consuming smell*. If there are words for it, they would be words I'd rather not know. Orders were confusing and contradictory. At times, our brigade did not even know whose command it was under. Decent billets were nonexistent. The meticulous Major got lice from sleeping in trenches and on dirty straw with no opportunity to change clothes or wash. He didn't complain though. He knew our regular soldiers had been suffering these vermin since Salisbury Plain and had always felt for them in that regard.

A lieutenant from the 10th Battalion came by and asked if The Major would be able to treat one of his soldiers with an eye injury. The man had gotten a fine metal splinter in his eye from a high-explosive shell. The Major said he would see what he could do.

Who was it? None other than Private Red Hay from Alberta. It was great to see him again and he seemed fit, except for the eye injury. The Major had him lie on the back of a wagon and look up into the sun, which was the best we could do for light. Then The Major used his magnifying glass and was able to extract the sliver with a pin and tweezers. He put a patch on it and told him to try to keep it covered for at least a couple of days if possible. We all knew that if he went straight back into the fighting, he wouldn't do this, but he said he would try.

"And where's our lacrosse-stick grenade-launching pal, Crowshoe?" The Major asked as Red stood up.

Red's visible eye became glassy and he covered it with his hand. The Major put his hand on Red's shoulder and squeezed.

"I'm sorry, son."

"Kitcheners Wood. Those goddamn machine guns."

The Major's eyes widened. "You were in that battle?" Red nodded. "Good Lord. Did you ever hear what General Foch said? He called it the finest act of the war."

Ferdinand Foch was a French general.

"I heard that. Didn't seem too fine when we lost three quarters of our men, and our Colonel Boyle to boot." Red shook his head sadly. "Colonel Boyle. Why did he turn that flashlight on? Why would he do that, Major?" Red's voice rose with emotion. "Make himself a target like that. He was an experienced soldier." Red shook his head.

This was detail he hadn't known of. The Major struggled to find words.

"Just the same," The Major said solemnly, "I am honoured to know someone who fought in that battle, Private Hay." The Major extended his hand and they shook.

"I better get back," said Hay.

"Godspeed, son," said The Major. "Take good care." Private Hay nodded, awkwardly felt his eye patch, put his wedge cap back on his red head and off he went.

A couple of days after Private Hay left, we made friends with a lovely little Irish terrier. She was a feisty, funny little character who would steal Dodge's leather blacksmith gloves and shake them furiously. We were so happy to have a dog around. Then she was run over by a supply wagon, badly wounded in her back and had to be shot. We all felt the loss of her, and I thought to myself, "It's terrible how quickly one can become attached to a new friend like that. In war, you just can't count on anything. It's tempting to close your heart and become hard."

After that event, with a look of complete resignation, The Major sighed heavily and said, "I suppose it's just a tiny tragedy in a very large theatre of misfortune."

One interesting thing did occur here though. There was increasing murmuring and talk in the ranks about that poem The Major had written during the battle in Ypres, the poem called, "In Flanders Fields." The Colonel was said to have rescued the poem, on a crumpled piece of notepaper he found by the canal.

The Colonel said, "It is a poem literally born of blood and fire. The soldiers have not only memorized it, they have learned it with their hearts."

**

At the end of May, The Major got orders to leave Festubert and the artillery. He was to go on leave in London and then join the CAMC (Canadian Army Medical Corp). He had been promoted to Lieutenant Colonel and Doctor in Charge of Medicine at the new McGill war hospital that had been such a contentious issue earlier on. As with everyone in the CAMC, he would now be under the command of General Carleton Jones.

Although everyone congratulated him roundly on his promotion, my blood ran cold. All I could think of was, *What will become of me, when he leaves?*

We rode out to the batteries and said our goodbyes to everyone. He was loathe to leave his very dearest friends: The Colonel and Captain Cosgrave. Nothing can ever compare to friendships forged in war. Nothing. He felt sick about leaving them and worse, leaving them in such a hot zone of battle. But orders are orders.

The Major left me with Dodge in Chocques, France. He gave me a hug and assured me that he'd send for me as soon as the new hospital was set up. I gave him one of my famous and best lip-waffling kisses on the forehead, which always made him laugh. Dodge assured him that I would get the best of care, and I knew this was true. Then he set sail for England.

As I watched him leave in a motorcar for the ferry, I was filled with anxiety, the fear that we would be separated as per the ever-present threat: medicals are not allowed mounts.

My darkest fear soon turned out to be well-founded.

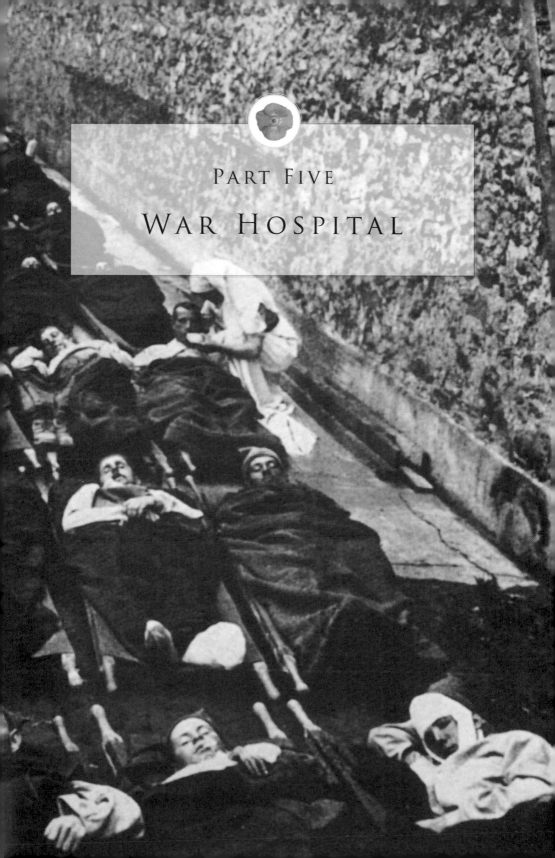

PART FIVE

WAR HOSPITAL

THIRTEEN

What most people did not know about The Major was that he had always hoped to stay in the artillery and command his own battery. Colonel Morrison wanted this too, and had tried to arrange it at the beginning. But The Major was simply too valuable as a doctor, and a doctor with military experience was even more valuable yet. It would never be allowed.

It made me heartsick to think that he was now permanently away from his best friend, Colonel Morrison, and now under the command of General Jones. The bad blood was deep between these two men and went all the way back to South African days, although I never learned the specifics. I did hear The Major deride the so-called hospitals in the Boer War as disgusting and disgraceful and badly run. He said that more men had died of dirty water and poor hygiene than of actual war wounds. He was also uncomplimentary about the medical corp in general and that seemed to carry right over into this war. Now he was to be part of it.

Well, Dodge and I would do our best until we could be together with The Major again. We could only hope. The brigade was in battle, and Dodge and I were safely behind the lines. Because of being in action, there was no one to exercise me by riding out, so Dodge just led me for a walk every day. These walks were not long or far though because he was nervous of both shell and gunfire. He was mortified of anything happening to me in The Major's absence, especially after my close call in Ypres. The Chestnut Gentleman was soon bored. Boredom would have been preferable to what happened next.

A young captain whom we didn't know appeared at our stable one morning with a scrawled, handwritten order stating that he was to take possession of me. Dodge went frantic and told the man this could not be correct and he would need to speak to The Colonel and that I belonged to The Major. The captain did not like Dodge's insubordination, but he also seemed bemused. He hadn't known that there would be any sort of fuss or controversy. I wondered who had put him up to this, or led him on. I thought I might have an idea.

He grumbled but agreed to come back the next day. He said that Dodge had better get the matter sorted out immediately because he didn't have time to waste, and if Dodge did not have an order to the contrary in the morning, he would be leaving with me.

As soon as he left, Dodge tried to find The Colonel but was told he was up at the front lines. Then he searched for Captain Cosgrave and was told he was in a battle zone and inaccessible. Needless to say, the two of us did not sleep a wink. The next morning, Dodge led me out for my walk. He just didn't know what else to do. We hoped maybe the man would come and then leave while we were gone. We returned before lunch and no sign of him. So far so good.

Dodge had just given me a bucket of water when the captain appeared. "Well, Private? My unit is leaving in half an hour. Do you have something to countermand this?" He held up the handwritten order and waved it back and forth.

"No, sir," stammered Dodge. "But . . . but . . . " Dodge looked around for someone, anyone from our brigade, but everyone was engaged in intense fighting at the front. We were on our own.

"But nothing. I'm taking this horse for my mount and that's that. Tack him up. Now."

Dodge stood there for a moment, crestfallen. Then he slowly turned and gathered my saddle and bridle. He whispered, "Don't you worry, Master Bonfire. We'll get this sorted."

The captain asked curtly, "Are you having a conversation with that horse? Just get a move on, Private."

Dodge tacked me up and the man got on. He pulled my head around roughly and then jabbed me in the ribs with his spurs and, well, I wasn't used to that sort of rough treatment at all, so I leapt forward and he almost lost his seat.

"Dammit," the captain said. "What sort of ill-trained . . . "

But before he could finish his sentence, a hand grabbed my reins. It was Cosgrave!

"Get off," he said to the stranger.

"By whose authority? I have an order here . . . " He fumbled for it in his tunic pocket with one hand, and Cosgrave held on.

Out of his own back pocket, Cosgrave produced another order, a telegram. He shook it out of its folds and held it up.

"Re: horse Bonfire STOP Order STOP Minister of War STOP horse stays with 1st Bde. STOP Sir Sam Hughes STOP," he said. He squinted at the other captain's order. "Fraid this trumps that, Captain."

I had never been so happy to see a soldier, other than The Major, in my life. The mystery captain jumped from my back and stormed off in a huff. And, after I'd taken his hat off and dropped it on the ground, I gave Captain Cosgrave one of my special gooey kisses right on the top of his head. Cosgrave chuckled, and I thought Dodge would faint with relief. I also offered a silent but very sincere prayer of thanks for that iron-jawed, blustery old Minister of War, Sir Sam Hughes.

* * *

When the train, with the freight car I was in, rumbled up near the new McGill tent hospital at Dannes-Camier, The Major was there to meet Dodge and me. I'd never ever seen such a broad grin on The Major. I jumped down out of my train car and The Major flung his arms around my neck.

"I knew they could never separate The Chestnut Gentleman from me." He tousled my forelock, and I reached out and took the swagger stick out of his hand. We walked to the hospital, and I carried his stick almost the whole way.

Dodge remarked, "Have you thought of teaching him to retrieve, Colonel?" and the two men laughed heartily.

I, myself, laughed quite heartily on the inside, without dropping the stick, of course. Oh yes, now he was a Lieutenant Colonel so I would have to think of him now as Colonel McCrae. The other Colonel, our Colonel Morrison, from whom we were now sadly and permanently separated, had been promoted to Major General. I would refer to him now as General Morrison.

We spent a few happy weeks at the tent hospital at Dannes-Camier, far from the firing lines. Bell tents again, for accommodation. I loved it there because nearly every day, following afternoon rounds, Colonel McCrae and I would ride to the ocean and sometimes, even go in. This was a novelty for me and after being a bit scared of it initially, I learned to really enjoy the soft sand and salty water.

Like everything in the military, it was not to last. When the fall came, so did terrible weather: winds, rain and snow. Shades of Salisbury Plain. The Colonel had rigged up a tent shelter for me, which I would dive into at the slightest sign of dirty weather. That fall we also received a disturbing note that Rudyard Kipling's son, John, had gone missing, presumed dead in the Battle of Loos. One never got used to hearing these sad messages.

A winter storm virtually destroyed our tent hospital. We had to move quickly, and we felt terrible for our injured patients, who had quite enough to deal with already. The day of the storm, many of them lay in their beds completely exposed to the weather after the tents had been torn up, and some entirely blown away, by the winds. It was awful.

A more suitable place for the hospital had to be found as soon as possible. An abandoned and partially burned Jesuit school was found further up the coast, near Boulogne. We took possession of it and moved in on January 7, 1916.

FOURTEEN

Although partially burned, much of the Jesuit school was intact. There were many outbuildings we could use on grounds that sprawled over almost twenty-six acres. We employed the use of bell tents again, but only in a minor way this time and it was nice not to have to depend on them. It was the perfect spot for the new No. 3 Canadian General Hospital (McGill).

So we settled into life at the hospital outside Boulogne and for once, things were actually constant for a good while. Colonel McCrae was Doctor in Charge of Medicine. Colonel John Elder, a gentle giant, was Doctor in Charge of Surgery and Colonel Herbert Birkett, with whom Surgeon General Jones had had such a fight earlier on, was the Commanding Officer.

I had a comfy stall in a small barn and, when I wasn't with Colonel McCrae, the almost undivided attention of Dodge. Colonel McCrae stayed in a lone bell tent, away from all the others, and right beside the little wooden hut he had turned into his pathology laboratory. Except for the daily arrival of wounded soldiers to look after, the war seemed far away.

Soon I became a favourite of the legion of nursing sisters, who would come by in twos and threes daily with ginger cookies, apples, carrots, sugar lumps and a certain kind of French flower that I liked to eat. I liked to lick the cookie crumbs and sugar off their hands, and one of the sisters, Sister Claire, a strawberry-blonde beauty with freckles and green eyes, exclaimed to my Master, "Look how he licks our hands, Colonel. He's just like a dog!"

I thought this was hilarious because no dog could ever be as big and beautiful as I was. There's no denying, I was spoiled rotten and about as happy as a horse can be.

Lieutenant Colonel John McCrae with Bonneau, Boulogne, 1916

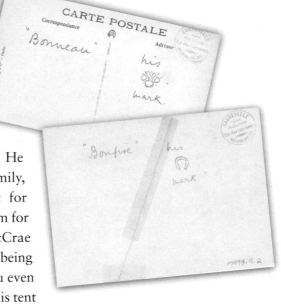

Speaking of dogs, within a short time, Colonel Mc-Crae and I were adopted by a wonderful canine friend. Bonneau was a liver-and-white French spaniel. He belonged to the Debakker family, the hospital's caretakers, but for some reason, he abandoned them for us. Bonneau and Colonel McCrae became inseparable. I admit to being jealous of that because Bonneau even got to sleep with my master in his tent and I was just a little too big for that!

Bonneau was a funny fellow because although friendly and playful, he had a serious way about him. When The Colonel occasionally took a cup of tea with Dodge in the barn, Bonneau would rest his head on The Colonel's knee, and look up at him with a most soulful expression.

"You are a very grave character, Bonneau," The Colonel would say with a chuckle, patting the spaniel's head, "and you conduct your canine business very gravely."

The Colonel wrote regular and amusing letters to his sister's children, his niece and nephews in Winnipeg, detailing the exploits of Bonfire and Bonneau. He would ask silly questions of them such as, "Do you like to eat your carrots with their tops on?" and, "How do you like your oats? Out of a bucket or out of a manger?" Then he would sign the letters as us, with a hoof print for me and a paw print for Bonneau. I thought this was exceedingly clever, and I was sure the children got a huge kick out of it.

Every night after rounds Colonel McCrae and Bonneau would come and get me, and we would ride out somewhere peaceful. Usually we rode down the Valleé Denacre in the deeply forested hills on the edge of town. A gurgling stream ran alongside the trail. Sweetly singing birds filled the air with their exuberant chorus. The Estaminet du 2me (short for Deuxieme) Moulin, a café where Colonel McCrae would sometimes take his dinner, was a special place along the stream with a waterwheel beside it. It had been a mill in times past.

This all sounds idyllic, but there were troubling signs with Colonel McCrae's health and his mood. The battles at Ypres and Festubert were still very much with him. If he was not distracted by pressing tasks at work, or riding out with me and playing with Bonneau, dark thoughts would invade him, and you could see it. Like an awful shadow they would descend over him.

He often began to talk to me as he would his human friends. That is, of more serious matters than he used to express to me before. He stopped singing his song about the minstrel boy, too. One evening after he took his dinner at the Estaminet du 2me Moulin, we returned to the hospital as darkness descended. As we clopped down the road onto the hospital grounds, he sighed with his whole self and slumped in the saddle.

"God I hate this place . . . and this war," he said, and rested his head on my neck. "Bonfire, I find it hard to believe now that I ever wanted to be a soldier. I would never have dreamt I'd get it in such overmeasure."

Bonneau and I did our best to entertain him. Bonneau would bring him sticks or his ball to throw. And me, I would carry his hat or his swagger stick, or pull on his pockets, which usually yielded some hidden treasure: an apple, a sugar lump or cookie. The trail in the Valleé Denacre was lined with blackberry bushes, and when they were in season, Colonel McCrae would pick them by the hatful and the two of us would eat our fill. Those were the happiest times.

Bonneau was a great talker, and if Colonel McCrae prompted him at all, he would lift his muzzle up and make all kinds of wonderful sounds, usually finishing with an extravagant, "Whoooo woo wooo," which our Master loved to hear. Bonneau would go with The Colonel on rounds, and the patients loved him. It always did their poor hearts good to have a cuddle with that kindly liver-and-white spaniel. Occasionally he would carry a bone or a stick the whole way round. The officious Matron MacLatchy, who was in charge of all the nursing sisters, watched, but to her credit, resisted the urge to call an end to it. She could see the good it did the wounded men.

I didn't get to meet the patients indoors but outside was another matter. I got all the attention I could stand, not only from the nursing sisters but also from the staff, and the patients too. At least the ones who were well enough to be out on the grounds.

One day when Colonel McCrae was busy inside, Dodge led me around the grounds to eat my fill of grass. This was one of my favourite pastimes. The Colonel often said I was the most industrious grazer he'd ever known. On this day four Australians came up and asked for Colonel McCrae. They wanted to meet the writer of the famous poem.

One of them, a huge, burly character with a thatch of blonde curls and his arm in a sling, said with his heavy Aussie accent, "We know who Bonfire here is, but who the hell are you?" which made Dodge laugh, in spite of their rudeness. Then that soldier put his face up to my nose, and I gave him my best waffly kiss, right on the lips. His friends broke up laughing.

One of them said, "That's the best kiss you've had since we left Australia, mate."

* * *

An ambulance truck came into the hospital on another afternoon when Dodge and I were walking about the grounds. A sergeant who had been unloading the wounded ran to Dodge and asked, "Where is Colonel McCrae? We've got a special case for him."

Dodge said, "I'm pretty sure he's in the pathology lab."

"Thanks," said the sergeant, and he took off at a dead run for the lab.

Dodge and I walked to the area where the wounded were coming in, and in no time, we knew what the sergeant had been talking about. There, together on one stretcher on the ground, was a little English Tommy (Tommy was a nickname for a British soldier), and a big, black mongrel dog, who was wounded as well. The Tommy had awful stomach wounds and the dog's back leg was shattered.

A few minutes later, Colonel McCrae appeared with Bonneau behind him, and he leaned down to the soldier and his dog.

"Well, well. What have we here? How are you, son?" The Major asked the Tommy who we came to know as Private Will Potter of the 1/Lincolns.

"Not too well, Colonel. Got shot in the gut. But I'm more worried about me dog, 'ere." He put his arm around the big mongrel and squeezed the dog to him. "This 'ere's Windy, an 'e's been over the top with us twice. See these two ribbons on his collar? 'E's been wounded twice too. And now his leg is buggered. Can you patch 'im up, Colonel? E's me best pal."

"I'll patch the two of you up, don't you worry." Colonel McCrae stood up and spoke to two orderlies. "Take Potter here to Ward C and take Windy to my tent. Put him on Bonneau's bed beside the stove."

Colonel McCrae gently patted the black dog on his massive head, and Windy licked the Colonel's hand. Bonneau sat nearby and looked quite miffed at this huge, black interloper who was now going to take his bed, but I knew he'd get over it. Bonneau's heart was as big as our Master's.

Colonel Elder, the Chief Surgeon, went to work on Will Potter and found that his wounds were quite terrible and complicated. Stomach wounds usually were. But he was holding his own for now and actually seemed to improve after a couple of days.

Windy, on the other hand, was in Colonel McCrae's hands. By the end of the day, The Colonel had done a minor surgery, inserted a small steel pin into his leg, and put him in a cast from the top of his foot almost to his hip. Within a couple of days, he was limping along behind Colonel McCrae and me and Bonneau. We all became friends with Windy, and the big fellow was a welcome addition to our little family.

His master, Will, had seemed to be healing up nicely when he took an awful turn for the worse. The decision was made to ship him to England as soon as possible. This coincided with an order to quickly vacate as many patients as could be moved. It was the end of March 1917, and a huge offensive had been planned for Vimy Ridge. No. 3 Canadian General Hospital (McGill) had to clear out beds to make way for new waves of wounded that would be arriving once that battle was underway.

The Colonel was sure that Windy would be able to go home to Blighty with his master, but the brass hats did not agree and, in fact, refused to allow it due to quarantine restrictions. As I've said, nothing brings creatures closer than war. We all knew this, and to see Will Potter denied was heartbreaking. Even Colonel Elder tried to help, but the brass in charge would not be moved.

A tearful Will Potter was loaded back on a hospital train bound for the coast without his dear dog, and all Colonel McCrae could do was apologize and assure him that Windy would always have a loving home with us.

* * *

Well, old Windy had a bad habit that came to light once his cast was off and he was fully mobile. He thought anyone who was not in uniform was a slacker. In fact, he did not like anyone in civilian attire and would bite without provocation. This discovery was not made until he, unfortunately, demonstrated this proclivity. We were all in the yard that day, Bonneau, Dodge and me, too.

The fat, cranky, stubble-faced milk delivery man whom The Colonel had had words with before due to milk that had gone off turned up in the yard one day with a large wooden crate full of milk. As he struggled across the yard toward the kitchens with his heavy load, Windy spied him and made a run at him before Colonel McCrae even realized what he was doing. Growling, Windy bit the man's leg first and drew blood. Then he got hold of the man's tweed pant leg and would not let go. The crate flew out of the man's hands, and milk bottles went every which way. Some landed on the grass and several shattered on the cobblestones. Bonneau happily began to lick up the spillage.

Colonel McCrae came running and grabbed Windy by the collar and hollered, "Windy, stop." He yanked the dog away, and the milkman swore a blue streak of French obscenities which, fortunately, none of us understood. A blood stain spread out on the milkman's trousers around the calf, and The Colonel slapped his hand to his head.

"Je suis désolé, monsieur," which meant he was sorry.

The milkman stormed off angrily, still swearing.

Colonel squatted down and patted Windy. Bonneau came and sat beside them for moral support.

Colonel McCrae, Pvt. Herbert Cruickshank, Bonfire (with his tongue stuck out), and Bonneau, 1917

"Dog! What are you trying to do? Good Lord. You can be sure we haven't heard the end of this. Now, you're going to have to be tied up from this day on, and if there's one thing I hate, it's tying dogs up."

* * *

The Battle of Vimy Ridge began, and I didn't see much of my Master for awhile. The hospital was inundated with casualties, many of whom ultimately did not come through. The Colonel made sure everyone had proper medication and also pitched in for surgeries when the surgical staff was overwhelmed. His devotion to the soldiers was absolute.

It was a fantastic victory for Canada. What the French and British had failed to do in three previous efforts– dislodge the Germans from this very strategic place–the Canadians had finally succeeded in doing. For the first time, all four Canadian divisions had fought together under our Canadian commander, General Arthur Currie. Some say Canada's identity as a nation was forged that day and she came of age as a nation of her own.

I was at the barn with Dodge when an excited Colonel McCrae came by with a letter from General Morrison. He read parts of it to us. General Morrison had written that it was the greatest day ever for the artillery and everything had gone like clockwork. It was a masterpiece of planning and strategy.

He read, "The only thing that could have made it more perfect . . . " and here, Colonel McCrae's voice caught in his throat. He began again, "Morrison says, 'It could only have been more perfect if you'd been with us.' And then he says, 'This is history as she is made, not as she is writ!'"[1] He chuckled at this and looked up at us. "If I'd been with them," he said, and smiled wistfully through tears. "If only . . . " his voice trailed off.

* * *

The days wore on and the winter was particularly cold, and hard on Colonel McCrae. Still, he insisted on staying in the little bell tent beside his pathology lab. Colonel Birkett, Colonel Elder and even Head Matron MacLatchy tried in vain to get him to move into a more comfortable hut. But he wouldn't have it. His asthma flared up, almost surely exacerbated by several gassings in Ypres. He developed a jarring, almost constant cough, a bark, he called it.

One of the more distressing pathologies he had to treat was an awful thing called gas gangrene, a muscle tissue infection that actually gave off a foul gas. This infection was thought to be a result of wounded soldiers having to lie for any length of time in the heavily manured Flanders fields. One of the ingredients in the manure cocktail was human waste, which The Colonel thought disgusting.

He became irritable at times. One day, a New Zealand soldier in a wheelchair on the lawn called him Doctor McCrae, and he uncharacteristically snapped at the man. "Do not call me doctor, boy. I am a soldier. You will call me Colonel McCrae!"

As for remaining in the bell tent, he said stubbornly, "I will not stay in quarters that are better than our soldiers in the field."

One day when I was out with Dodge, I overheard Colonel Birkett say to Colonel Elder in exasperation, "What are we going to do about McCrae? I had to pry him out of the artillery uniform, order him out of it. And now this. Staying in that blasted bell tent. Aaagh. This . . . this . . . it's martyr behaviour!"

And then Colonel Elder said something that shocked me. He referred to another doctor friend and colleague of Colonel McCrae's from

---

1. Graves, Dianne. A crown of life: the world of John McCrae/Dianne Graves — St.Catherines, Ont. : Vanwell Pub., c1997. — xx, 300 p., [8] p. of plates : ill., map, ports,; 24 cm. — ISBN 1550680919, quote, "This is history as she is made, not as she it writ!" Edward Morrison to JM, 11 April 1917, GM Papers

Montreal, who currently worked in a war hospital in England—Eddie Archibald. Before the war, The Colonel had had an apartment in Doctor Archibald's house for eight years, while he taught pathology at McGill.

"You know, Eddie says Jack was . . . is . . . badly shell-shocked."

Colonel Birkett seemed taken aback and calmed down. He looked over his glasses at Colonel Elder. "You don't say. Does he really think that?"

"He really does," said Colonel Elder, "and so do I."

* * *

In the fall of 1917, the hospital was ordered to vacate patients again. As many as were well enough to be shipped off to England had to make way for the casualties of the next big offensive: the 3rd Battle of Ypres, or what we Canadians would know as Passchendaele.

The offensive began in late August, and the casualties swamped the hospital from the beginning. The Colonel was gone all day, every day, and when he finished at the hospital, he often didn't have the energy to ride out with me. I treasured the times that he did. Those days we always went down the Valleé Denacre. It was the most private and secluded of our places, and the place he began to prefer more and more. Bonneau came with us, but Windy had to be tied up or on a leash, so Dodge gave him his exercise.

Late one night after an extremely busy day of work, The Colonel came back to his tent and saw Windy's collar and chain were there with no dog attached to them. The Colonel was just too tired to worry about it. He went into the bell tent and fell into a deep sleep. At first light, he and Bonneau heard a dog whining outside. Colonel McCrae went out and there was Windy, lying on his side with white froth coming from his mouth.

Colonel McCrae quickly determined that he'd been poisoned, probably with strychnine. There was nothing he could do but give the poor dog morphine to ease his pain until he died. And that's what he did. He stoked up the stove in his bell tent and sat on the floor with Windy's head in his lap. Every time the dog's pain returned, he would give him a shot of morphine until finally, Windy, the faithful war dog of the 1/Lincolns, who had been over the top twice and now had three wound stripes on his collar, succumbed to poison. We thought we knew who had done it, but there was no proof. Just another casualty of war.

Windy was buried with a little ceremony and a proper wooden cross. All The Colonel said was, "How I hate to lose the faithful beasts."

* * *

The weeks wore on, and casualties of Passchendaele came in non-stop. In the first week of November, in dreadful wet, cold weather the Canadians finally took Passchendaele Ridge, and that was the end of it. Colonel McCrae was in the yard, directing the field ambulance to the spots where the various wounded men would be treated, when he saw a tuft of bright red hair under a bandaged head go by on a stretcher.

He called out, "Private Hay, is that you?"

Private Red Hay told the stretcher bearers to stop, and Colonel McCrae walked up. "Set him down for a minute, boys." The Colonel kneeled down beside him. "We meet again, Private. Were you with the 10th when they took the ridge?" He took Red's hand.

Red Hay smiled weakly. He got up on one elbow and whispered, "I was, sir. It was a dirty day, but a great day. But I don't think I'm going to make it this time, sir." He fell back down. He was covered from head to foot with yellowy-gold mud and blood. "It was terrible out there, Colonel. The worst I seen in this whole war. Men that weren't even hurt bad just sunk into the muck and disappeared. And horses . . . and mules." He closed his eyes and shook his head, like he could see it all again.

I shuddered at the mention of mules and hoped that Magnus and Monty had made it through.

The wounded had to wait outside. Because of the crush of new casualties, space had to be made inside, so The Colonel waited with Red. Red's eyes opened and he spoke, barely above a whisper. "Colonel . . . Sir . . . we learned your poem. Would you say it?"

Colonel McCrae seemed taken off guard by this and shook his head. His eyes were bloodshot and he looked suddenly so very tired.

Now there were three rows of soldiers on stretchers: Canadians, Australians, New Zealanders, a couple of kilted Scots. All had wounds of varying severity and all waited to be brought inside. Nursing sisters bustled about with piles of blankets and made sure they were all well covered as it was a chilly November day.

Briefly energized, Red asked again. "Colonel McCrae, would you say the poem, sir? Please. It would mean so much to me." He strained to look around at the other men. "To all of us."

"Private, I really can't . . . I . . . "

"Please, sir," he implored, and squeezed the Colonel's hand.

Dodge and I stood nearby, and Dodge began to get misty-eyed.

The Colonel stood up amid the mass of stretcher cases and closed his eyes. Quietly he began, "In Flanders Fields the poppies blow, / Between the crosses, row on row, / That mark our place; and in the sky / The larks, still bravely singing, fly, / Scarce heard amid the guns below. / We are The Dead . . . " his voice trailed off and he whispered, "I can't. I can't do this."

At which point a Scottish accent piped up, "We are The Dead. Short days ago / We lived, felt dawn, saw sunset glow, / Loved, and were loved, and now we lie, / In Flanders Fields."

Colonel McCrae looked around in amazement.

Then a few more voices, all from the other stretcher cases, took it up. "Take up our quarrel with the foe: / To you from failing hands we throw / The torch; be yours to hold it high. "

And here, The Colonel quietly spoke the last words, along with the soldiers and some nursing sisters, too.

"If ye break faith with us who die, / We shall not sleep, though poppies grow / In Flanders fields."

He exhaled with a sigh and looked down at Red Hay. He was gone. Matron MacLatchy strode over quickly and pulled the blanket up over Private Hay's face. She motioned a couple of stretcher bearers to take him away and they moved quickly. The Colonel stood motionless.

Then Colonel Elder appeared in the doorway and said, "Alright, bring this lot in. We've made space."

Colonel McCrae gathered himself and carried on with the work. Dodge led me back to the barn and put me in my stall for the night.

* * *

On January 24, 1918, Colonel Elder found Colonel McCrae sleeping heavily in a chair in the officers' mess. This was most unlike him. You could hear his breathing and it wasn't good–rasping, squeaking, crackling. He woke him up and asked him if he was alright. He said he was, but Colonel Elder was very concerned.

Later that night he became very ill and vomited repeatedly. The next day he seemed to improve, but now he became concerned that he might have pneumonia. At the same time, Colonel Elder told him that he had been promoted to Consulting Physician of the First Army for the British. This was a huge honour, especially for a Canadian, and showed how much respect he had as a doctor. The Colonel was well pleased with this news.

But the next day, he spiked a high fever and it was clear he had developed severe pneumonia. After trying to treat him at No.3 and not seeing any improvement, Colonel Elder had him moved to No.14 in Wimereux, the British Officers Hospital. He desperately thought it might have the very best standard of care, even though No.3 Canadian General Hospital (McGill) was well known to be excellent. By late afternoon Colonel McCrae became paralysed down one side of his body and lapsed into a coma.

That afternoon, Major General Morrison appeared in the barn. This was quite unexpected as he'd never come by the hospital but once before. I was happy to see him. He patted me on the neck and then spoke to Dodge. They walked away down the barn aisle and had a confidential-sounding chat. Mainly, General Morrison spoke while a somber Dodge listened and nodded and said, "Yes, sir." I heard my name mentioned more than once and something about "back with the brigade." It frustrated me that I couldn't quite hear it.

In a few minutes they returned to me. General Morrison scratched my forehead. "Dear old Bonfire. I wish I'd come by more often," he said.

He kept fussing with his left breast pocket, feeling it and lifting and closing the flap. Paper rustled each time he did it.

"Forgive me, sir," said Dodge, "are you missing something, or . . ." Dodge gestured toward his pocket.

General Morrison paused, and then opened the pocket flap and withdrew a small, stained, worn out piece of paper with faint pencil writing on it.

"It's an early draft of the poem. I found it by the canal during the battle. He'd written several, as you do. I've kept it here ever since." He patted his left pocket, his heart, and put it back in.

General Morrison began to walk out when he stopped, and turned to us again.

"That dog, Private, what's his name again? Bonhomme?"

"It's Bonneau, sir."

"Well, he was sitting in the middle of the road to Wimereux when we came in. We had to drive around him. You might want to tie him up, or put him in a stall or something, before he gets run over."

Of course tying Bonneau up was not an option.

After General Morrison left, Dodge went out and found Bonneau exactly where The General had said. He was sitting in the middle of the road to Wimereux, where he waited for our Master's return. Dodge had to forcibly bring him to the barn and put him in the stall beside me, for his own safety. Then he lied down with his face between his paws and looked up at me with the gravest of expressions.

* * *

That night Dodge and I were on pins and needles. Dodge did not sleep at all, nor did I. Nor did Colonel Elder. I stood in the corner of my stall, nose to the wall, while Dodge worked around me with the fork, mucking out and fussing with the straw, even though it was perfectly clean at this point.

"Got to have your stall spotless, Master Bonfire. Don't want to get a blast from The Colonel when he comes back to us."

Suddenly I smelled my Master's pipe tobacco. I had my nose in the corner and immediately nickered a greeting as I turned around. I walked to the stall door, hung my head out and looked down the aisle toward the barn door he normally came through.

"What is it, Bonfire?" asked Dodge. He looked down the barn aisle, too. There was no one there. Then he looked at his watch. "One thirty a.m." He looked at me. "I smell his pipe, too." Then he shuddered. "Crikey. I just got a chill."

The next morning, Dodge and Colonel Elder stood in the hallway outside Colonel Elder's office by the phone and waited for news. It rang at five thirty in the morning, and Colonel Elder snatched it off its cradle.

Funeral of Lieutenant Colonel John McCrae,
Wimereux, France, 29 January, 1918

"Yes?" His shoulders fell. "Yes. I see. Yes. I'll start making arrangements." He hung up.

Colonel Elder was a huge man, and Dodge looked up at him hopefully. The colonel closed his eyes, dropped his head and shook it from side to side.

"He left us at one thirty this morning. I can't believe it. Jack is gone. All my friends are dying, Private Dodge."

The two men went in separate directions, both blubbering like children. Their hearts were broken, and so was mine.

* * *

January 29 was a magnificent day, the first beautiful day in a long while. Unseasonably warm and sunny. You could see the English Channel to the west. The funeral for Lieutenant Colonel John McCrae was one of the biggest in all of World War One. There were many soldiers, officers and dignitaries, and all the nursing sisters came with their white headdresses flying out behind them in the sea breeze.

They all paraded through the village of Wimereux from No.14 British Officers Hospital to the communal cemetery of Wimereux. Colonel McCrae's casket was on a gun carriage draped with a Union Jack. General Currie was there, the commander of all the Canadians, and he walked with my Master's dear friend, Major General Morrison. Dodge led me in the procession with my Master's boots reversed in my stirrups. Even as I walked, I could hardly imagine that I would never see my Master ever again. It was certainly the greatest honour

Private William Dodge holding Bonfire with Colonel McCrae's boots reversed, 29 January, 1918

of my life to have this duty. It was also the saddest day of all my days.

Canon Almond said the eulogy, and it was very moving. The canon had known The Colonel for many years in Montreal. His voice broke repeatedly. He had to really work at composing himself. Colonel Elder stood with his hat over his face and his great shoulders shook. In the whole crowd, I did not see a dry eye. A bugler played "The Last Post" and as they lowered Lieutenant Colonel Jack McCrae down, as if on cue, the distant sound of artillery came into voice. We would never see such a man again.

I, Bonfire, former Fox Hunter Extraordinaire, and now a bona fide war horse, would open myself up to what fate had in store for me. In honour of my Master, whom I would hold in my heart forever, I would serve with devotion, wherever the call was loudest.

EPILOGUE

lthough *Bonfire — The Chestnut Gentleman,* is a work
of fiction, it is based on over six years of exhaustive research and several trips to Flanders. I wanted to know
as much about the man, his times and the war as I could
before telling the story. In getting to know John McCrae, I wanted, as
much as possible, to rely on his own words, the accounts of people
who actually knew him personally at the time and my own impressions
of the places where he had lived, travelled and experienced the war.

In Flanders, Belgium and northern France, I wanted to see what he
had seen, smell what he had smelled and experience the landscape as
well as I could without being on horseback, as they were much of
the time. To this end, in the summer of 2011, I rode a motorcycle
from where his brigade landed at St. Nazaire, France, to Steenwerck,
where they detrained, to Meteren, where they stayed with the elderly
French ladies, and then into Belgium and through Oudezele, where
they billeted after Fleurbaix, their first battle, to Ypres, where their
second battle was fought and the poem was written and finally to
Wimereux, where John McCrae died and is buried. As I rode, I tried
to imagine what it must have been like for them–young Canadians
from diverse backgrounds, most of whom had no experience at all
of war and no idea what to expect.

For dramatic purposes, time is telescoped in places, some events are out of sequence and dramatic licence was taken with some of the smaller, personal events inside and outside the scope of the war. The sequence of the larger events is factually accurate: Valcartier, Salisbury Plain, Neuve-Chappelle, the 2nd Battle of Ypres, Festubert and No. 3 Canadian General Hospital (McGill). Alexis 'Lex' Helmer and Owen Hague were blown up by the same artillery shell, and Helmer's death prompted the writing of the poem, "In Flanders Fields." Bonfire's pen-mate was actually killed by a shell too, only mere feet from him and he did escape to safer ground. The title of Part Four, Cometh the Night, is taken from a line in an earlier poem McCrae wrote about death in 1913, called The Night Cometh.

The horror of Festubert, France, in May/June 1915 added insult to injury after their bloody stint beside the Yser Canal in the 2nd Battle of Ypres. In his own diary of May 29, 1915, McCrae wrote about how the place was scattered with unburied or partially buried dead bodies, broken equipment, water-logged trenches, shell holes and ground scarred in all directions "in bewildering disorder."[1] Festubert was an intense battle zone, and in another diary entry, May 27, 1915, he mentions getting a "blacksmithing from heavy guns [that] drew a perfect hornet's nest about our heads."[2] He was anxious and sad to have to leave his friends in this violent battle zone when he was removed from the artillery.

Bonfire was taken away from McCrae after the two battles but returned to him after he joined the McGill hospital through no small amount of string pulling and interventions.

In one instance, I have combined two actual people to make one character and that is Dodge. Dodge is a composite of McCrae's two loyal

---

1. 29 May 1915

2. 27 May, 1915

servants, Herbert Cruickshank of Banff, Scotland, McCrae's batman and groom in the artillery and CAMC, and William Dodge, who served him after the battles while he was with the CAMC. Dodge was originally from Portsmouth, England but settled in Verdun, Quebec and returned there after the war. These men served both McCrae and Bonfire, too, with love and devotion. Alberta privates, Lionel Crowshoe and Red Hay are fictitious characters representing the large group of soldiers who made up the Fighting 10th Battalion from Calgary and Winnipeg areas. Hundreds of First Nations soldiers served in World War One from across Canada. Two of the most famous snipers in the war were Native Canadians, Henry Norwest from Alberta and Francis "Peggy" Pegahmagabow from Ontario. The latter was possibly the most prolific Allied sniper in the entire war.

Bonneau was probably returned to the hospital caretakers, the Debakker family. There was a rumour that he was later stolen by gypsies! The story of Windy the war dog of the 1/Lincolns is true and was learned of from Major Harvey Cushing's WWI memoir, From a Surgeon's Journal. Cushing was an American neurosurgeon at the Harvard war hospital in France and had been a colleague of McCrae's under Sir William Osler during Johns Hopkins days in 1899.

Major General Sir Edward Morrison, Captain Lawrence Moore Cosgrave and Lieutenant Alexis Hannum Helmer, were actual people and among John McCrae's closest friends during the war. McCrae and Morrison had the longest friendship and actually did meet Rudyard Kipling in South Africa in 1900 when they were young lieutenants in the artillery. They also did have lunch with him fourteen years later on Salisbury Plain.

Major-General Sir Edward Whipple Bancroft Morrison, one of Canada's great "gunners" of WWI, died in 1926 and is buried in Beechwood Cemetery in Ottawa. I have been part of a small group and initiative to have his gravestone there restored. There is a Mount Morrison in southern Alberta named after him on the Smith-Dorrien

Highway. (Horace Smith-Dorrien was also a World War One general from England.) Alexis H. Helmer, as we know, died in The 2nd Battle of Ypres and his name is engraved on the Menin Gate in Ypres/Ieper along with the thousands of names of those with no known grave. Because where Helmer fell is known, there are people who want to have a gravestone erected in the Essex Farm Cemetery for him along the Yser Canal. "The Baby," Lawrence Moore Cosgrave, went on to have a long career as a diplomat and represented Canada in World War Two in taking the surrender of the Japanese aboard the *USS Missouri* in 1945. Owen Hague who was hit by the same shell that killed Alexis Helmer, was invalided out but died of his wounds a few days later. He is buried in Hazebrouck, France, just below the Belgian border.

The son and only child of McCrae's medical mentor, Sir William Osler, and Grace Revere Osler, joined the army initially as a quartermaster. Edward 'Revere' Osler had known John McCrae since he was a child and I believe he was much impressed by McCrae's military tales and stories of artillery exploits in South Africa. He was soon bored with his cushy job as quartermaster and went to great lengths to get himself in the Royal Artillery. He was killed in August of 1917 at age twenty-two in the early fighting of 3rd Ypres or Passchendaele. He is buried in Dozinghem Cemetery in Belgium. Sir William never recovered from Revere's death. I'm sure also that news of young Osler's death would have been a devastating blow to McCrae.

There is a mystery concerning Bonfire's fate that I hope to get to the bottom of some day. One account has him being sold after McCrae's death and then retired somewhere in northern France. Then, it is said that McCrae's mother, Janet, who received the proceeds from the sale, donated the money to a campaign to build a monument to her son in Wimereux, France. I find this unlikely because I don't think Bonfire was hers to sell.

Another story has Bonfire being given to Lieutenant Colonel Bartlett McLennan of the 42nd Battalion, Canadian Black Watch, who was killed in action shortly thereafter on August 3, 1918.

Bonfire was given to McCrae as his charger by McCrae's McGill colleague and horseman, Doctor John Todd. Another account states that after McCrae's death, Todd's wife, Marjory, who was an avid and accomplished horsewoman, wanted the horse back and believed that he was coming back. She was told he would be arriving on a ship in Montreal and went to the docks to meet it. Once all passengers and cargo had come off the ship, there was, to her dreadful disappointment, no sign of Bonfire. For me, this is where the trail goes cold. I hope to solve the mystery of Bonfire's fate some day.

In any case, almost every diary entry and letter written by John McCrae during the war mentioned Bonfire and his antics, and later, when he was in Boulogne, Bonneau the dog, too. He was, all his life, an avid lover of horses, dogs, cats and children. He wrote in a letter that Bonfire was the dearest thing one could ever hope to find in a horse. He referred to Bonfire and Bonneau as "his little family" in the months before his death, and I think they were his lifeline to decency and sanity, especially in those last awful years of the war.

Horses and mules served in great numbers throughout the war. Millions of horses died in World War One. They hauled field guns and pulled ammunition and supply wagons. They were ridden as cavalry horses in the last and more mobile weeks of the war. Soldiers loved their horses and mules and were often just as devastated by the deaths of these animals as they were by the deaths of their human comrades. Some of the horses who survived the war were brought home if they were lucky enough to be owned by senior officers. Most of them were shot and butchered for meat at the end of the war to feed the hungry and destitute citizens of Belgium and France.

Imagine those teams and drivers who brought ammunition to McCrae and his brigade. During the 2nd Battle of Ypres, the road beside the canal was continuously swept with shellfire and bullets. In his diary of the battle on April 25, McCrae wrote, "The good old horses would swing around at the gallop & and then pull around in an instant and stand puffing & blowing, but with their heads up, as if to say, 'wasn't that well done!' It makes you want to kiss their dear old noses & and assure them of a peaceful pasture once more.'"[3] They were absolutely essential to the war effort.

Dogs were also used, and McCrae gave safe-haven to two dogs during the 2nd Battle of Ypres. One, he wrote on May 9, was "a small black & white dog, with some tan spots," who ran into his dugout during a fierce bombardment, "& going to the farthest corner [the dog] began to dig furiously. Having scraped out a pathetic little hole 2" deep, it sat down and shook, looking most plaintively at me."[4] The harm done to animals weighed heavily on McCrae, not just the trauma the soldiers and civilians suffered.

At the time of this writing, in 2012, much has been learned again about the effects of war trauma on those who serve. I say "again" because this invisible wound is as ancient as humanity itself and was always recognized by warrior cultures such as the ancient Greeks, who called it nostalgia, and by many Native American nations. Called shell shock in World War One, it has had many names over the millennia: soldier's heart in the Civil War, battle fatigue in World War Two, PTSD or post traumatic stress disorder after the Viet Nam War. It's finally starting to be understood that this type of trauma, what Canadians now call an operational stress injury or OSI, can be every bit as damaging as a bullet, albeit an emotional or moral injury or a wound of the soul rather than the body. It can be just as debilitating and often even harder to recover from because there is nothing visible to treat.

---

3. 25 April, 1915 &

4. 9 May, 1915 - LAC, MG30, D209 - John McCrae Collection, War Diary 1915 22 April - 5 June

John McCrae's quick decline after the battles he was in is almost certainly due, in large part, to combat trauma. One of his best friends from Montreal, surgeon Eddie Archibald, stated with certainty that his friend, Jack, was "badly shell-shocked." Another woman who knew McCrae in Montreal before the war, saw him on leave in France after the 2nd Battle of Ypres, and was rocked by his appearance. She said that he had aged twenty years. In my own research, I was jolted by the photographs of him, by how fast he went from a handsome, vital young man to someone who looked like his own father in the space of about two and half years.

It's hard to know just how profoundly The Great War has shaped the character of our nation. Out of a nation of a mere eight million people at the time, about sixty-six thousand men were killed. That's sixty-six thousand devastated families and friends. Then there were the hundreds of thousands of men and women who returned with catastrophic injuries, both physical and emotional. How did they affect their families, their children?

John McCrae's legacy is a simple, heartfelt poem, written in the middle of a terrific battle that captured the hearts of soldiers at the time, and still moves people almost a hundred years later. This poem is also the reason we wear the poppy in all the Commonwealth countries every November. Inspired by McCrae's poem in 1915, an American professor from Georgia, Moina Michael, who volunteered helping American World War One veterans, conceived the idea of using hand-sewn cloth poppies to raise funds for disabled veterans and also as a universal symbol of Remembrance. The idea took off in the commonwealth countries especially and was popular in the U.S. at the time, but eventually lost its appeal there. Surprisingly, there are many people who wear the poppy every November who don't know its origin as the symbol of remembrance.

In June 2011, I rode my motorcycle to Wimereux, France, and the communal cemetery where John McCrae is buried. I was moved and amazed by the tributes I found there around his gravestone, ninety-three years after his death. There were small crosses, English and Canadian poppies and a tiny Canadian flag. He still matters. Remembrance and the honouring of those who have served us is still important.

The causes of World War One are many, complicated, and I make no effort to explain them here. Men and women left their Canadian homes to serve for many reasons: for adventure, for the pay, out of a sense of duty, out of a sense of honour as subjects of the British Empire. I also believe there are those for whom being a warrior, with whatever it brings, is as much a calling as being a concert pianist. Ideally, warriors are guardians and protectors and actually going to war is a last resort.

Whatever the causes of war and whatever the reasons they served; they fought and suffered, sacrificed and died and those who returned were changed forever. Their lives and deaths matter. They were sons, daughters, sisters, fathers, grandfathers, husbands, brothers, uncles; the living fabric of our nation.

The veterans of The Great War have all died. Now the remaining veterans of World War Two, in their eighties and nineties are leaving us daily. We also need to be aware that there are veterans around us right now in their twenties, thirties and every age in between. They belong to us and we to them. For those who return, we need to help them shoulder the burden of what they've had to see, hear and do in our names. We mustn't break faith with those who serve us.

Let us go forward and be decent and good citizens in our country and on this precious earth. And for the fallen, whether they died in Flanders, or on the Falaise Road in World War Two, or in Korea or Yugoslavia, or the Panjwaii Valley of Afghanistan, let us never forget them. Let us be grateful for every day and for the wonderful country they have left us.

Let us be worthy of them.

Suggested Reading

John McCrae: An Essay in Character - Andrew Macphail, 1919, available on the internet

In Flanders Fields: The Story of John McCrae - John F. Prescott ©1985, Revised edition 2003, Guelph Historical Society

A Crown of Life: The World of John McCrae - Dianne Graves, © 1996, Vanwell Publishing Ltd.

With the Guns (In South Africa) - Edward W.B. Morrison, ©1901, Distributed by Eugene G. Ursual, P.O.Box 8096, Ottawa, ON Canada K1G 3H6

Welcome to Flanders Fields:The First Canadian Battle of the Great War, Ypres, 1915 - Daniel Dancocks, ©1988. Toronto: McLelland and Stewart

Three Day Road, a novel by Joseph Boyden, © 2005, Viking Canada

Ghosts Have Warm Hands - Will R. Bird, © 1968, Clark, Irwin &Company, CEF Books

The Great War as I Saw It - Frederick G. Scott, © 1999, CEF Books

No.3 Canadian General Hospital (McGill) 1914 - 1919 - R.C. Fetherstonhaugh, ©1928, Copyrighted by the Medical Faculty of McGill University

From a Surgeon's Journal - Harvey Cushing, © 1936, Little, Brown, and Company

The Life of Sir William Osler - Harvey Cushing, © 1940, Oxford University Press

William Osler: A Life in Medicine - Michael Bliss, © 1999, University of Toronto Press

At the Sharp End: Canadians Fighting The Great War 1914 - 1916, Volume One - Tim Cook, © 2007, Viking Canada

Shock Troops: Canadians Fighting The Great War 1917 - 1918, Volume Two - Tim Cook, © 2007, Viking Canada

Baptism of Fire: The Second Battle of Ypres and the Forging of Canada, 1915 - Nathan Greenfield, © 2007, HarperCollins Publishers Ltd.

Victory at Vimy: Canada Comes of Age: April 9 - 12, 1917 - Ted Barris, © 2007

Vimy - Pierre Berton, © 1986, Pierre Berton Enterprises

Bonfire Reference Materials

John McCrae Collection, MG 30, D 209, Library and Archives Canada

Works Cited

The Minstrel Boy

   approx. 1798, words by Thomas Moore, music - Traditional Irish air, The Moreen

It's a Long Way to Tipperary

   1912, by Jack Judge and Harry Williams

Drink to Me Only with Thine Eyes

   1616, words by Ben Jonson from his poem, To Celia. Music, traditional English folk song.

149

Credits

Permission to reproduce the following photographs is gratefully acknowledged.

Note: Canadian War Museum (CWM); Library and Archives Canada (LAC); William Okell Holden Dodds Collection (WOD) University of Victoria, In Flanders Fields Museum in Ieper, BE (IFFM).

Front Cover

M1968X_448_1 John McCrae, Bonfire and Bonneau, Guelph Museums

Back Cover

Two Men in Uniform, (John McCrae at Valcartier September 17, 1914), WOD Collection, "Scrapbook," Courtesy University of Victoria
Bonfire Illustration by Penny Corradine

Part One

Page VIII: WOD Collection, University of Victoria - horse lines at Valcartier

Page 15: photograph of Sir Sam Hughes on a postcard, courtesy private collection of Jim Keller

Page 17: Archives of Manitoba - Captain Colebourn and Winnie the bear N10471. Winnie was brought to England as a mascot by the Canadian Army Veterinary Corps, and ended up in the London Zoo where she inspired the Winnie the Pooh books by A.A.Milne.

Page 27: WOD Collection, University of Victoria - John McCrae at Valcartier 1914

Page 30: WOD Collection, University of Victoria - artillery column Valcartier

Part Two

Page 33: Glenbow Archives NA 4927-1 - 10th Battalion (from Calgary and Winnipeg) on Salisbury Plain, England

Page 37: Queen's University - 1st Brigade loading Saxonia

page 47: LAC, PA-22705, Mudlarking on Salisbury Plain

page 55: Guelph Museums, Cosgrave, Alderson and McCrae @ The Ark in Devizes, England

Part Three

page 58: Map Illustration of The Western Front by Marika d'Ailly

page 59: LAC, PA107276, Canadian Soldiers in France, 1915

page 63: CWM, 20020045-2882, 1st Brigade CFA on steps of The Bear Inn, Devizes, England

page 75: snowdrops in France, courtesy Susan Raby-Dunne

page 79: WOD Collection, University of Victoria, Sam Hughes with the MacAdams shovel

Part Four

page 82: CWM, 19700140-077, Gas Attack on the Somme

page 85: artillery on the move, photo by Frank Hurley - courtesy www.greatwar.nl

page 94: Essex Farm bunkers, courtesy Pierre Vandervelden www.inmemories.com

page 98: IFFM, Ieper, Belgium - Coll. Fhr von Kanne, aerial photo of the Yser Canal and position of 1st Bde. CFA.

** NOTE: This photograph is thought to have been taken approximately April 27, 1915, five days into the 2nd Battle of Ypres, because of its known number in a sequence, all of which were shot before 1 June, 1915. I think this is possible too, because of the minor shell damage in the photo at this point. It is thought that the cemetery I have an arrow pointing to, could be the Marengo Farm graves, but those were from after the 2nd Battle of Ypres. According to John McCrae's diary, "our plots fill up rapidly." It is possible, even likely, that the plots McCrae refers to were blown out of the ground in the course of the battle and those men have their names engraved on the Menin Gate, as does Alexis Helmer, even though where he fell is known. In any case the position of the 1st Brigade CFA during the battle is precisely known, and this location is correctly noted on the photograph.

page 101: LAC, PA-31000314 Cloth Hall in 1916

Part Five

page 110: M1972_5_4_page_56 - Stretcher Cases, Guelph Museums

page 120 : M1998_9_1 John McCrae and Bonneau, Guelph Museums

page 121: M1998_9_1_back, M1998_9_2_back, postcards with Bonfire and Bonneau's marks, Guelph Museums

page 123: Estaminet 2me Moulin, Boulogne, France, photograph by Susan Raby-Dunne

page 127: M1998X_8_1, McCrae, Cruickshank, Bonfire and Bonneau, Guelph Museums

page 136 : M1972_5_5_2, John McCrae's funeral, Guelph Museums

page 138: M1972_5_5_1, Dodge holding Bonfire at funeral, Guelph Museums